YORK NOTES

THE CRUCIBLE

ARTHUR MILLER

NOTES BY DAVID LANGSTON AND MARTIN J. WALKER

 Longman

 York Press

The right of David Langston and Martin J. Walker to be identified as
Authors of this Work has been asserted by them in accordance with
the Copyright, Designs and Patents Act 1988

YORK PRESS
322 Old Brompton Road, London SW5 9JH

PEARSON EDUCATION LIMITED
Edinburgh Gate, Harlow,
Essex CM20 2JE, United Kingdom
Associated companies, branches and representatives throughout the world

First published 1997
This new and fully revised edition first published 2002
Sixth impression 2006

10 9 8 7 6

ISBN-10: 0-582-50627-1
ISBN-13: 978-0-582-50627-5

Designed by Michelle Cannatella
Illustrated by Chris Price
Typeset by Land & Unwin (Data Sciences), Bugbrooke, Northamptonshire
Produced by Pearson Education Asia Limited, Hong Kong

CONTENTS

PREFACE

York Notes are designed to give you a broader perspective on works of literature studied at GCSE and equivalent levels. With examination requirements changing in the twenty-first century, we have made a number of significant changes to this new series. We continue to help students to reach their own interpretations of the text but York Notes now have important extra-value new features.

You will discover that York Notes are genuinely interactive. The new **Checkpoint** features make sure that you can test your knowledge and broaden your understanding. You will also be directed to excellent websites, books and films where you can follow up ideas for yourself.

The **Resources** section has been updated and an entirely new section has been devoted to how to improve your grade. Careful reading and application of the principles laid out in the Resources section guarantee improved performance.

The **Detailed summaries** include an easy-to-follow skeleton structure of the story-line, while the section on **Language and style** has been extended to offer an in-depth discussion of the writer's techniques.

The Contents page shows the structure of this study guide. However, there is no need to read from the beginning to the end as you would with a novel, play or poem. Use the Notes in the way that suits you. Our aim is to help you with your understanding of the work, not to dictate how you should learn.

Our authors are practising English teachers and examiners who have used their experience to offer a whole range of **Examiner's secrets** – useful hints to encourage exam success.

The General Editor of this series is John Polley, Senior GCSE Examiner and former Head of English at Harrow Way Community School, Andover.

The authors of these Notes are David Langston MA, English teacher and examiner at GCSE and 'A' Level; and Martin J. Walker, English teacher, journalist and senior examiner in GCSE English and English Literature.

The text used in these Notes is the Heinemann Plays edition, edited by Maureen Blakesley, 1992.

PART ONE

INTRODUCTION

HOW TO STUDY A PLAY

Though it may seem obvious, remember that a play is written to be performed before an audience. Ideally, you should see the play live on stage. A film or video recording is next best, though neither can capture the enjoyment of being in a theatre and realising that your reactions are part of the performance.

There are six aspects of a play:

❶ THE PLOT: a play is a story whose events are carefully organised by the playwright in order to show how a situation can be worked out

❷ THE CHARACTERS: these are the people who have to face this situation. Since they are human they can be good or bad, clever or stupid, likeable or detestable, etc. They may change too!

❸ THE THEMES: these are the underlying messages of the play, e.g. jealousy can cause the worst of crimes; ambition can bring the mightiest low

❹ THE SETTING: this concerns the time and place that the author has chosen for the play

❺ THE LANGUAGE: the writer uses a certain style of expression to convey the characters and ideas

❻ STAGING AND PERFORMANCE: the type of stage, the lighting, the sound effects, the costumes, the acting styles and delivery must all be decided

Work out the choices the dramatist has made in the first four areas, and consider how a director might balance these choices to create a live performance.

The purpose of these York Notes is to help you understand what the play is about and to enable you to make your own interpretation. Do not expect the study of a play to be neat and easy: plays are chosen for examination purposes, not written for them!

CHECK THE FILM

If you are unable to see *The Crucible* performed on stage, the film version on video is the next best thing.

AUTHOR – LIFE AND WORKS

1915 Arthur Miller is born in New York

1934–8 Studies at the University of Michigan

1940 Marries Mary Slattery

1944 *The Man Who Had All The Luck* is staged on Broadway

1945 *Focus*, a novel, is published

1947 *All My Sons* is staged

1949 *Death of a Salesman* premiers

1953 *The Crucible* opens

1955 *A View from the Bridge* is staged

1956 Divorces Mary; marries Marilyn Monroe

1957 Convicted of contempt of Congress for failing to name possible US Communists

1961 Divorces Marilyn Monroe; *The Misfits*, a film, premiers

1962 Marries Inge Morath; Marilyn Monroe dies

1964 *Incident at Vichy* and *After the Fall* are staged

1968 *The Price* premiers

1972 *The Creation of the World and Other Business* opens

1987 Publishes autobiography *Timebends: A Life*

1991 *The Ride Down Mt. Morgan* opens

2002 Inge Morath dies

Arthur Miller continues to be the foremost playwright of the USA.

CONTEXT

1914–18 First World War

1930s The great depression in America: there is widespread poverty

1939–45 Second World War

1944 Franklin D. Roosevelt dies; succeeded as president by Harry S. Truman

1948 Cold War begins (and lasts till 1989)

1950 Senator Joseph McCarthy begins his campaign against Communism within the US State Department

1950–53 The Korean War

1953 Stalin dies in Russia

1954 McCarthy is condemned by Congress

1959–75 Vietnam War

1961 John F. Kennedy becomes president

1963 Martin Luther King makes his 'I have a dream' speech; John F. Kennedy is assassinated and succeeded by Johnson

1964 Civil Rights Act enacted, prohibiting segregation

1968 Bobby Kennedy and Martin Luther King are both assassinated

1969 Neil Armstrong is the first man to walk on the moon; Nixon becomes president

1974 The Watergate Scandal: Nixon resigns, succeeded by vice-president Ford

1977–2002 Presidencies of Carter, Reagan, Bush, Clinton and Bush Junior

SETTING AND BACKGROUND

ARTHUR MILLER'S BACKGROUND

Early life

Arthur Miller was born in New York on 17 October 1915 and was brought up in the Brooklyn area of that city. His father was a clothing manufacturer whose small business collapsed in the financial depression of the 1930s, a period when many people like him went bankrupt.

After leaving school Miller worked for two years in a car parts warehouse to make enough money to pay for higher education. At the University of Michigan he won an award for his first play, a comedy, *The Grass Still Grows*. Miller completed his college course and continued to write although he worked at various manual jobs to earn a living. He had some success with radio dramas and in 1944 his play, *The Man Who Had All The Luck*, was performed on Broadway. This did not make much money but it won him New York's Theatre Guild Award.

Dramatic success

Miller's first real success was *All My Sons*, about a father who is forced to realise the dangerous moral compromises he has made in chasing the American Dream of wealth. He provided defective engine parts for the air force during the war and could have been responsible for the deaths of pilots, including his own son. Miller's biggest theatrical hit and his most highly acclaimed work was *Death of a Salesman* (1949) which won him, among other awards, the Pulitzer Prize. Willie Loman, the central character, is destroyed by his dependence on the false values of the business world to which he has devoted his life.

The Crucible won awards in 1953 but was not an immediate commercial success. However, Miller continued to write social dramas. *A View from the Bridge* (1955) and *After the Fall* (1964), which deals with some aspects of his unhappy marriage to the film actress Marilyn Monroe, are among the more successful of these. In 1960 he wrote a screenplay for *The Misfits*, a film which starred Marilyn Monroe and in 1996 completed a screenplay for a film of *The Crucible*, starring Daniel Day-Lewis and Winona Ryder.

CHECK THE NET
Search for Arthur Miller at **www.bbc.co.uk** and read more about his life.

DID YOU KNOW?
Two of Arthur Miller's plays, *Death of a Salesman* and *A View from the Bridge*, are set in Brooklyn, where Miller grew up.

DID YOU KNOW?
The salesman, Willie Loman, is perhaps Miller's best-known character.

Arthur Miller has continued to be a major dramatist. He has always been ready to deal with difficult and controversial issues and has tried to make his audiences consider both unpleasant and uplifting aspects of human behaviour.

WITCHCRAFT

DID YOU KNOW?

Many of those accused of witchcraft were old women.

For many hundreds of years throughout Europe there was a belief in witchcraft. At times this belief developed into hysterical fear, leading to campaigns of persecution against suspected witches. Some of them might have had a knowledge of herbal medicine or other folk remedies. Superstitious people would assume they had magical powers or were in league with the devil. In a time of fear it would be easy to accuse someone you did not like and very difficult for the accused to prove their innocence.

DID YOU KNOW?

King James I of England wrote a book on witchcraft.

Some scholars became experts in witchcraft and believed they knew how to identify witches. It was thought that witches were agents of the Devil and that they could change their shape. Many thousands of people accused of being witches were tortured and executed throughout the Middle Ages and up to the seventeenth century. The authorities used the text from Exodus, 22: 18 to justify these killings: 'Thou shalt not suffer a witch to live'

SALEM, MASSACHUSETTS

This belief in witchcraft persisted among the English colonists in America. In 1692 there was an outbreak of accusations of witchcraft in Salem, Massachusetts. The colonists there were Puritans who followed a particular form of Protestant Christianity and would tolerate no other. They felt surrounded by ungodly people and associated the forest with savages and with evil. Two young girls had been taking part in magic ceremonies. Ministers, doctors and magistrates were called in and soon accusations were multiplying. Before the panic had burned itself out, twenty people had been executed (one man was pressed to death by stones) and about two hundred had been accused. Later some of the witnesses and judges who had been involved publicly regretted what had taken place.

THE COLD WAR

In modern times the term witch-hunt has come to mean the searching out and persecution of religious or political dissidents, i.e. people who have views which are different from those of the majority and who may be considered a threat to the community. After the Second World War, relationships between the United States and the Soviet Union deteriorated and there followed a period known as the Cold War. Many people in the States feared that the Russians were aiming to take over the world. This led to a fear of Communism in the United States of America.

McCARTHYISM

Senator Joe McCarthy organised a twentieth-century version of witch-hunting. In the early 1950s he exploited the US fears about Communism and managed to create a national campaign against Communists. As chairman of a senate committee, the House Un-American Activities Committee, he interrogated many witnesses and tried to make them inform on friends and colleagues. Powerful figures like J. Edgar Hoover, the Director of the FBI, were happy to support McCarthy.

These included well-respected writers and film-makers. *The Crucible*, whose subject is the Salem witch trials, was first produced in 1953. This was when McCarthy's anti-Communist campaign was at its height and there are obvious parallels in the play: unsupported accusations; people encouraged to denounce their friends and acquaintances; a spiral of fear and suspicion.

McCarthy's unproven accusations and aggressive interrogations gradually brought him into disrepute. In 1954, after it had been shown that he and his associates had been falsifying evidence, he was removed as chairman of the committee. However, the witch-hunt continued for some years and Arthur Miller himself was called in front of the committee in 1956. Miller refused to give the names of friends who might have been interested in Communism and he was fined for contempt of Congress. Miller himself has tended to play this down.

CHECK THE NET

The Cold War can be seen in detail at **cwihp.si.edu/ default.htm**

CHECK THE BOOK

The Scarlet Letter by the American writer, Nathaniel Hawthorne, published in 1850, is set against a background not dissimilar to *The Crucible* – that of seventeenth-century Puritan Massachusetts.

DID YOU KNOW?

The Crucible was first perfomed in 1953 in the midst of anti-Communist hysteria.

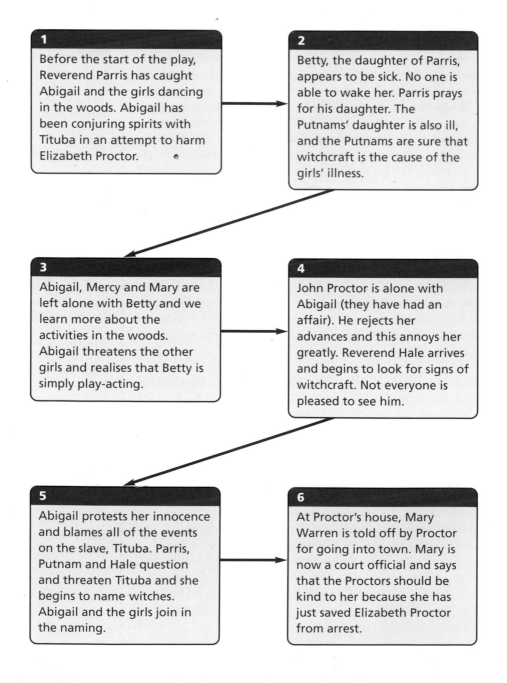

1
Before the start of the play, Reverend Parris has caught Abigail and the girls dancing in the woods. Abigail has been conjuring spirits with Tituba in an attempt to harm Elizabeth Proctor.

2
Betty, the daughter of Parris, appears to be sick. No one is able to wake her. Parris prays for his daughter. The Putnams' daughter is also ill, and the Putnams are sure that witchcraft is the cause of the girls' illness.

3
Abigail, Mercy and Mary are left alone with Betty and we learn more about the activities in the woods. Abigail threatens the other girls and realises that Betty is simply play-acting.

4
John Proctor is alone with Abigail (they have had an affair). He rejects her advances and this annoys her greatly. Reverend Hale arrives and begins to look for signs of witchcraft. Not everyone is pleased to see him.

5
Abigail protests her innocence and blames all of the events on the slave, Tituba. Parris, Putnam and Hale question and threaten Tituba and she begins to name witches. Abigail and the girls join in the naming.

6
At Proctor's house, Mary Warren is told off by Proctor for going into town. Mary is now a court official and says that the Proctors should be kind to her because she has just saved Elizabeth Proctor from arrest.

7
Hale arrives and wants to know if the Proctors are good Christians. Then Elizabeth is arrested because of a doll that Mary has brought into the house. In fact, Abigail is using the doll as 'proof' of witchcraft, in order to bring harm to Elizabeth.

8
In court, Proctor attempts to defend his wife and says that Abigail has been pretending witchcraft. Many people have now been arrested, some even sentenced to death. Mary changes her testimony and confirms Proctor's evidence.

9
Although she knows differently, Elizabeth tells the court that her husband has not been involved with Abigail. At this point Abigail leads the girls in a hysterical performance and Proctor is arrested.

10
Hale tries to persuade the prisoners to confess to witchcraft, and thus save their lives. Proctor is imprisoned and tortured but refuses to confess to witchcraft. Elizabeth finally persuades him to confess.

11
During his confession, Proctor sees Rebecca Nurse as she is about to be hanged. She has refused to confess to witchcraft, as she knows such a confession would be a lie. Proctor refuses to link his friends with witchcraft.

12
When Proctor is told that his confession must be displayed in public as a warning to others, he tears it up. He does not want to lose his good name. Because he has refused to confess, Proctor is hanged.

PART TWO

SUMMARIES

GENERAL SUMMARY

ACT I

In Salem, 1692, some girls have been caught dancing in the forest. The younger girls are frightened and pretend to be ill. The town's minister, Parris, is worried that word will get out that his daughter Betty and his niece Abigail were among the girls. He is worried for his reputation. The Putnams arrive at Parris's house and are pleased to find that the minister's daughter is ill. They jump to witchcraft as an explanation. This suits the Putnams as they are interested in revenge on their neighbours, including Parris who was appointed to the position that a relation of the Putnams wanted.

John Proctor is left alone with Abigail and she tries to rekindle the affair she had with him when she was the servant in his house. He refuses her advances and she loses her temper, mentioning that she blames his wife, Elizabeth.

CHECK THE FILM

It is well worth seeing the film of *The Crucible* (1997) starring Daniel Day-Lewis and Winona Ryder, for which Arthur Miller wrote the screenplay.

Betty wakes up and screams, bringing the others back into the room. Reverend Hale, a famous witch-finder, arrives and begins to look for signs of witchcraft in Betty Parris. When Abigail is asked about the dancing and conjuring in the forest she blames the black slave, Tituba, who she says bewitched her. Tituba is questioned and quickly becomes confused. She merely repeats whatever suggestion is put to her and ends up confessing to having dealt with the devil. Abigail joins in with the confession and both women call out the names of people from the town whom they have seen with the devil.

ACT II

Eight days later, the Proctors' servant, Mary Warren, has become an official of the court appointed to look into the rumours of witchcraft. Many more people have now been accused. Elizabeth wants her husband to go to the court and denounce Abigail, who is clearly behind the accusations. He reluctantly agrees to go, but Mary Warren returns and brings Elizabeth a poppet. Shortly afterwards, Hale arrives and questions the Proctors as to the Christian nature of their home. Officials from the court bring a warrant for the arrest of Elizabeth, and they have been instructed to search the house for poppets. They find such a doll with a needle stuck in its belly. This resembles the way that Abigail found herself to be stabbed with a needle that same evening. Elizabeth is arrested.

ACT III

Giles Corey goes to court to try to save his own wife and Proctor arrives to present evidence that Abigail and the girls have been lying all along. He has persuaded Mary Warren to tell the truth about the girls but she is very nervous at the prospect. When Danforth, the deputy governor, seems to doubt Abigail (on the testimony of Mary Warren) Abigail pretends that Mary is sending her spirit out to attack her. Proctor stops this by confessing that he had an affair with Abigail and that the girl is simply trying to kill his wife out of jealousy.

Elizabeth Proctor is brought in and questioned, but she defends her husband's good name, even though she does know of his affair. Hale believes Proctor, and Danforth is starting to listen to reason when Abigail screams that she is being attacked by a bird sent by Mary Warren. The girls join her in crying out against Mary. This frightens the girl so much that she sides with Abigail and says that Proctor is the Devil's man. Proctor is arrested and Hale denounces the court, realising that justice has not been done.

ACT IV

On the morning of his execution, Proctor is given a last chance to confess to witchcraft and so save his life. He is allowed to speak to his wife and decides that he will confess. He refuses to allow his signed confession to be posted on the door of the church as he does not want his friends and family to think badly of him. He chooses to allow his execution to go ahead rather than give up his good name.

EXAMINER'S SECRET
Remember: simply re-telling the story is not a high-level skill.

Now take a break!

Detailed summaries

pp. 1–5 – An overture

❶ The character of Parris is introduced.

❷ We hear about the town of Salem and its inhabitants.

❸ We learn that the play will be about a witch-hunt.

DID YOU KNOW?

Many people fled to America to escape religious persecution back in England and so the Puritan lifestyle was fiercely guarded.

After describing the room in Parris's home, Miller supplies some background information about the small town of Salem, Massachusetts.

Salem had been in existence for only forty years. Life in the small town was hard, and the strict religious code made it harder by forbidding any form of 'vain enjoyment' (p. 2) such as the theatre, singing or dancing.

People were expected to attend worship and there were special wardens appointed to take down the names of those who did not attend so that the magistrates could be informed.

> ### Reasons for the witch-hunt
>
> Salem was governed through a combination of state and religious power, 'a theocracy' (p. 4), in the hope of keeping evil at bay. As the times became less dangerous, the need for such strict rules lessened and people began to express an interest in 'greater individual freedom' (p. 5). The witch-hunt came about as people began to explore this freedom.
>
> The witch-hunt also gave people 'a long overdue opportunity' (p. 5) to revenge themselves upon old enemies and to settle old scores to do with land ownership. Some people used it as a way to free their consciences from sins they had committed, by blaming things upon innocent victims.

The land bordering Salem was largely unexplored, 'dark and threatening' (p. 3) and wild animals, along with marauding Indian tribes, posed a constant threat. This made many people conform to strict rules that they might otherwise have ignored.

pp. 5–14 – Betty is taken ill

❶ Parris prays for his daughter Betty.

❷ The doctor has suggested supernatural causes for the illness.

❸ Parris questions his niece Abigail.

❹ The Putnams visit; their daughter Ruth is sick too.

The play opens with Parris praying for Betty. Tituba, his black slave, enters. Parris brought her with him from Barbados where he used to be a merchant. Tituba is frightened by Betty's sudden illness. Abigail Williams, Parris's niece, enters and tells Parris that Susanna Walcott has arrived from Doctor Griggs. Susanna says that the doctor can find no explanation for Betty's illness in his books, but that Parris 'might look to unnatural things for the cause of it' (p. 7).

DID YOU KNOW?

Even devoutly religious people like Parris kept slaves during this period.

Parris is frightened and angered by this: he is already unpopular in the town and he knows that he cannot afford to be associated with any suggestion of unnatural events. Parris is shown as a miserable, harsh man who thinks that everyone else should be as serious as he is. This extends even to young children, whom Parris does not understand at all. He turns on Abigail and confronts her with the fact that he caught her, Betty and others dancing in the forest. Abigail admits to having danced in the forest but says 'when you leaped out of the bush so suddenly, Betty was frightened and then she fainted' (p. 7). When Parris caught the girls, Tituba was with them. Tituba was waving her arms, screeching and swaying over the fire.

CHECKPOINT 1

Do you think the involvement of Tituba and Abigail differs from that of the other girls?

Despite Parris's accusations of witchcraft, Abigail tells him that 'It were sport, uncle!' (p. 8). She knows she is close to being found out and tries to claim the girls' activities were innocent. Parris thinks he saw someone naked running through the trees, but Abigail denies this. Parris asks his niece why she was dismissed from Goody Proctor's service and why Goody Proctor says she will not come to church if it means sitting near something so soiled as Abigail. She replies that she was treated like a slave by Mrs Proctor and will not black her face for any of them. Abigail loses her temper and calls Goody Proctor 'a gossiping liar' (p. 9). Parris is very close to discovering the real reason that Abigail left Proctor's house. He is put off from doing so by the arrival of the Putnams.

The Putnams

The Putnams resent Parris and are deeply vengeful people. Thomas Putnam had opposed the appointment of the previous minister as he wanted his own brother-in-law to have the position. This resentment is carried over to Parris.

When Mrs Putnam enters, she is pleased that misfortune has befallen Parris. She has heard that Betty flew over Ingersoll's barn. Before Parris can refute this, Thomas Putnam enters. He ignores the minister and goes straight to the bed to look at Betty. He compares Betty with his own daughter who has also been taken ill. Mrs Putnam says that the girls are not merely sick, but that 'it's death drivin' into them, forked and hoofed' (p. 10). It is really Mrs Putnam's actions that lead to the suggestion of witchcraft. She does not see that her daughter was simply becoming an adolescent, but prefers to blame her change in behaviour on Ruth having been bewitched. Note her continuous alternation between rational and hysterical remarks.

The Putnams are delighted that Parris is in trouble. They might be able to replace him as minister and blame their own misfortunes on witchcraft at the same time. The Putnams deviously manipulate the situation for their own ends.

Despite Parris's denial that any witchcraft has taken place, he has sent for Reverend Hale of Beverly, a well-known expert in the 'demonic arts' (p. 10). Putnam sees this as an admission of the minister's guilt and says that the village must know of it. Mrs Putnam says that she lost seven babies shortly after their birth, and that her only child has been strange recently. Because of this she sent her daughter, Ruth, to see Tituba.

Mercy Lewis, the Putnam's servant, arrives. She says that Ruth has shown signs of improving. The Putnams leave with Parris, who has gone to pray with the crowd outside. Abigail and Mercy are left alone with Betty.

CHECK THE BOOK

The Chrysalids by John Wyndham (1955) is set in a future when any differences or mutations in plants, animals or humans are seen as works of the Devil.

Glossary

forked and hooved the devil was often thought to have a forked tail and cloven hooves

pp. 14–17 – Abigail, Mercy and Betty

1 We learn what the girls have really been up to in the forest.

2 Abigail threatens Betty, Mercy and Mary.

Mercy tells Abigail that Ruth's illness is 'weirdish' (p. 14). Abigail tries to wake Betty, and Mercy offers to hit the young girl to bring her round. Abigail tells Mercy that she has admitted to dancing in the woods and that 'He knows Tituba conjured Ruth's sisters to come out of the grave' (p. 14). Mercy also finds out that Parris saw her naked. Mary Warren, the servant of John Proctor, enters. She wants to tell the adults what the girls were doing in the forest and says that Abigail will only be whipped for what they did. Abigail tells Mary that if she is whipped then Mary will be too.

Betty wakes up, feels threatened by Abigail and asks for her (dead) mother. She then tries to climb out of the window but is pulled back by Abigail, who hits her. Betty has heard Abigail talking to Parris and knows that she has not told him everything: 'You drank blood Abby! You didn't tell him that!' (p. 15). Abigail did this in order to cast a spell to kill Proctor's wife. Abigail tells the girls that they are to admit to dancing and to conjuring Ruth's dead sisters but not to any of 'the other things' (p. 15). Mary Warren still wants them to own up to everything. Abigail is prevented from hitting her by the entrance of John Proctor.

CHECKPOINT 2

In what way is Abigail still rather innocent here?

The girls' true natures

Abigail and Mercy are genuinely puzzled and concerned by Ruth's condition. They have not yet grasped the seriousness of the situation. Remember that they are still quite young and have not yet become a part of adult society.

Abigail clearly frightens the other girls and they are prepared to do whatever she tells them. Abigail is obviously the ringleader and shows that she is able to keep her head in a difficult situation.

pp. 16–19 – Abigail and Proctor

1 Abigail is alone with Proctor, probably for the first time since their affair.

2 Abigail wants Proctor but he rejects her.

3 Abigail quickly turns against her former lover.

Proctor is in his mid-thirties and is a well-respected farmer. He is known for being strong and people are wary of him. Proctor scolds Mary for neglecting her duties and sends her home. Mercy Lewis also leaves, saying she has to look after Ruth. Abigail immediately flatters Proctor: 'Gah! I'd almost forgot how strong you are, John Proctor!' (p. 17). He has heard the rumours of witchcraft and Abigail says that it is all because her uncle caught her and some other girls dancing in the forest the night before. Proctor seems to encourage Abigail: 'Ah, you're wicked yet, aren't y'!' (p. 17).

Abigail tries to seduce Proctor, saying 'I am waitin' for you every night' (p. 17). He tells her that he never gave her such hope. She replies that she has more than hope and refers to her affair with him. Abigail condemns Proctor's wife for the end of the affair and says that she knows Proctor has been thinking of her. She clutches him and he

> **CHECKPOINT 3**
>
> How does Abigail's behaviour change when Proctor enters the room?

> **CHECKPOINT 4**
>
> How might Proctor be said to have behaved badly towards Abigail?

gently moves her aside. As he does so he calls her 'Child' (p. 18). This angers Abigail who tells him that, thanks to him, she is no longer a child. Abigail vows to act against Elizabeth Proctor, whom she calls 'a cold, snivelling woman' (p. 19). Proctor tries to leave, but Abigail rushes to him and begs him to take pity on her. Just then the sound of a psalm can be heard from outside and Betty sits up and calls out. The noise she makes brings Parris back into the room.

The end of the affair

Abigail's continued attraction to Proctor is one of the key driving forces behind events. They have had an affair and still feel a strong physical attraction for one another, as Abigail declares: 'you loved me then and you do now!' (p. 18). Proctor, however, has made up his mind that the affair with Abigail is over and he shows strength of character in refusing her. Abigail naturally feels abandoned by Proctor. It is now that bitterness sets in, and she begins to seek vengeance.

pp. 19–26 – Small-town politics

❶ The Putnams arrive and make the situation worse.

❷ Rebecca Nurse calms Betty.

DID YOU KNOW?

Not being able to bear to listen to prayer was thought a clear sign of being in league with the devil.

Parris, Mrs Putnam, Thomas Putnam and Mercy Lewis enter. It is a coincidence that Betty has cried out whilst a prayer was being said but Mrs Putnam says that the girl cannot bear to hear the Lord's name. Thomas Putnam adds 'That is a notorious sign of witchcraft afoot' (p. 20). Husband and wife seem delighted to be able to point the finger of suspicion at Parris.

Rebecca Nurse enters and Parris asks her to help Betty. Giles Corey appears and asks whether Betty is going to fly again. As Rebecca stands next to the bed, Betty becomes calm.

Feuding families

Miller tells us about the history of the Nurses and the Putnams:

- The Nurses had been involved in long-running disputes over land with a member of the Putnam family.

- It was the Nurse family who had prevented Putnam's brother-in-law from becoming minister.

- The Nurses had established their own township outside Salem and this was deeply resented by Putnam.

- The first complaint against Rebecca Nurse was signed by Edward and Jonathan Putnam and it was Ruth Putnam who pointed out Rebecca, in the courtroom, as her attacker.

CHECKPOINT 5

What do we learn here about Giles Corey?

Rebecca says that Betty will be fine if everyone leaves her alone. She knows that the little girl is frightened and looking for attention. Proctor backs her in this and challenges Parris over the fact he has sent for Reverend Hale. Proctor also argues with Putnam and says that the town should have been consulted before this step was taken: 'This society will not be a bag to swing around your head, Mr Putnam' (p. 22). Proctor is quick to see that Putnam is using the situation to try to further his own cause. His predictions of Putnam's intentions are frighteningly accurate. Putnam retorts by saying that Proctor has not been seen at church for some time. Proctor claims this is because he will not listen to the 'hellfire and bloody damnation' (p. 23) preached by Parris. Rebecca supports this allegation.

CHECKPOINT 6

How does Rebecca Nurse manage to cure Betty so easily?

Parris complains that the people of Salem do not respect him, and brings up the fact that he has not been supplied with firewood. Giles and Proctor remind him that he is paid a salary of £60 and given £6 more for firewood. Proctor also complains that Parris keeps asking for the deeds to the minister's house. Parris says that there is a faction in Salem opposed to him and Proctor adds that he would like to join such a faction. By setting himself against Parris at this early stage, Proctor unwittingly gives Parris and Putnam reasons to arrest him later on.

CHECKPOINT 7

What do Parris's complaints reveal about his character?

There is then a dispute between Giles and Putnam over land and Putnam threatens to take Corey to court. Giles has a reputation for filing law-suits and has even had Proctor fined recently. He says too much against Putnam here and so seals his fate.

pp. 26–40 – Reverend John Hale

1 Hale arrives and prepares to drive out the devil from Betty.

2 Giles Corey says too much and endangers his own wife.

3 Hale questions Abigail, who nearly cracks.

4 Tituba gets the blame and begins naming witches.

Hale is introduced; and in his long introduction, Miller draws parallels with the situation in America during the McCarthy era (see **Setting and background**). Hale believes himself to be an educated witch-finder. He thinks that he has all the Devil's ways accounted for in his books and sees the people of Salem as naive in their interpretations of evil. Hale takes the proceedings very seriously: 'He feels himself allied with the best minds of Europe' (p. 30). He is told the symptoms of Betty and Ruth, and Proctor says that he hopes Hale will bring some sense to the situation. Hale reprimands Putnam for saying that being

unable to bear to hear the Lord's name is a sure sign of witchcraft. Hale points out, 'We cannot look to superstition in this' (p. 31).

Hale is surprised to hear that the townsfolk allow dancing, and Mrs Putnam tells him that Tituba was engaged in magic. She is adamant that it was not natural for her to lose seven children in childbirth. Rebecca Nurse is '*horrified*', saying 'Goody Ann! You sent a child to conjure up the dead?' (p. 32). Rebecca leaves, quietly refusing to have anything to do with the proceedings. Hale prepares to exorcise the devil from Betty. Giles Corey interrupts and begins to ask questions about his own wife. Giles claims that his wife reads strange books and that this has stopped Giles from praying. Hale ignores him and concentrates on Betty, praying over her in Latin. Betty does not stir.

Hale questions Abigail as to what the girls were doing in the forest. Parris adds that he thinks he might have seen a kettle in the grass. When Hale asks him if there had been any movement in the kettle, Parris says there was. Abigail denies full participation but mentions Tituba, who is then sent for. Hale enquires as to whether Abigail had felt a cold wind or a trembling below the ground. Parris and Abigail take up Hale's suggestions. They hope that by agreeing with Hale suspicion might be lifted from them. When Hale presses Abigail, she insists 'I'm a good girl! I'm a proper girl!' (p. 35). However, Abigail

<aside>
CHECKPOINT 8

How is there a sign here that Mrs Putnam will later bring trouble to Rebecca Nurse?
</aside>

remembers much of the information about witchcraft that is given here. She will use this later, especially in the court scene.

DID YOU KNOW?

The behaviour described here was typical of voodoo ritual thought to be practised by slaves.

The interrogation

Tituba is brought in and Abigail accuses her of making her do it. She says that Tituba makes her drink blood, and the slave admits to giving the girls chicken blood. Abigail blames her wicked dreams on Tituba, and Hale tells the slave to wake Betty. Putnam threatens to have Tituba hanged and, as a result, Tituba is terrified and clearly willing to say whatever she thinks the men want to hear. In fact, most of what Tituba says is at the prompting of Parris, Putnam and Hale. This grows more pronounced as the interrogation goes on and she simply repeats the last thing that is said to her. Tituba mixes her feelings for Parris and her desire to return to Barbados with her statements about the Devil. She is clearly very confused, but the men are too excited to notice.

Hale asks Tituba if the Devil came alone or with someone whom she recognised. Putnam asks if he came with Sarah Good or Osburn. Parris presses her as to whether it was a man or a woman who came and Tituba says that they were all witches out of Salem. Hale tells Tituba that she has confessed and so can be forgiven. She says that four people came with the Devil and that the Devil tried to get her to kill Parris. Tituba names one of the people as Goody Osburn. Mrs Putnam seizes upon this information as Osburn was her midwife three times.

CHECKPOINT 9

Why are the names suggested to Tituba important?

At this point in the play, some of the characters are terrified whilst others are quick to exploit this fear for their own ends. Abigail, as though she is in a trance, adds the names of Sarah Good and Bridget Bishop to the list – the two young women suggested by Putnam earlier. Notice how the whole idea of naming townsfolk starts here. Betty simply becomes carried away; she cries out the names of George Jacobs and Goody Howe. Abigail is using this to divert attention from her own activities. The names of Martha Bellows, Goody Sibber, Alice Barrow, Goody Hawkins, Goody Bibber and Goody Booth are also cried out by Betty and Abigail. Miller is clearly using the situation as an **allegory** of the hysteria created during the McCarthy era. Note the power of suggestion in creating hysteria.

Mass hysteria

Abigail uses the confession of Tituba to divert attention from her own actions. She is soon caught up in the hysteria of the moment, albeit pretence on her part. At this point, Abigail realises the effect that strong emotions can have on a group of weak-minded people. It is here that she witnesses the unusual behaviour of several people who are carried along on a tide of hysteria and it is clear that her actions in Act III reflect this new knowledge.

CHECKPOINT 10

What dangerous Ideas is Abigail able to pick up here?

Now take a break!

WHO SAYS ...?

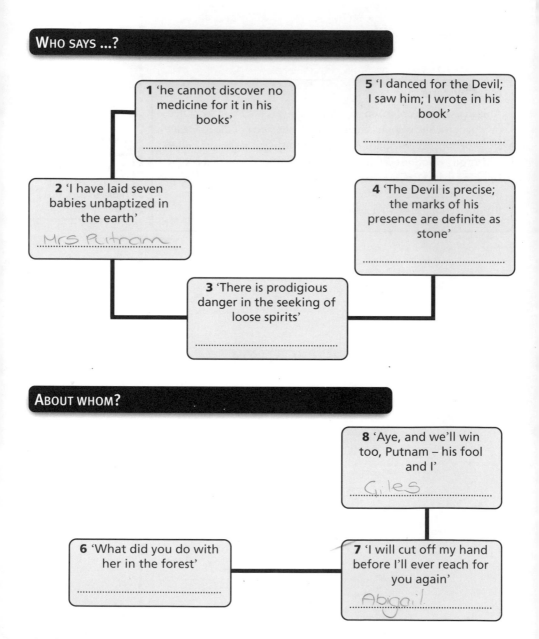

1 'he cannot discover no medicine for it in his books'

....

5 'I danced for the Devil; I saw him; I wrote in his book'

....

2 'I have laid seven babies unbaptized in the earth'

Mrs Putnam

4 'The Devil is precise; the marks of his presence are definite as stone'

....

3 'There is prodigious danger in the seeking of loose spirits'

....

ABOUT WHOM?

8 'Aye, and we'll win too, Putnam – his fool and I'

Giles

6 'What did you do with her in the forest'

....

7 'I will cut off my hand before I'll ever reach for you again'

Abigail

Check your answers on p. 72.

pp. 41–5 – John and Elizabeth

1. The relationship between John and Elizabeth has become strained.

2. Mary Warren is in court.

3. Abigail and the girls now have real power.

The Act opens eight days later, in the common room of Proctor's house. The stage instructions say that Proctor is not pleased with the food in the pot over the fire and that he meddles with it. This behaviour indicates that John and Elizabeth are not getting on so well as they might. Throughout the opening sequence, John and Elizabeth are distant from one another. They speak of the farm and the weather, but do not seem comfortable together.

Mary Warren has been in Salem all day. This is against John Proctor's orders, but Mary is 'an official of the court' (p. 43) trying people for witchcraft and so Elizabeth has let her go. There are now fourteen people in jail, who will be hanged if they do not confess. Elizabeth comments upon Abigail's new power and fame saying, 'where she walks the crowd will part like the sea for Israel' (p. 43). If Abigail and the girls scream and fall to the floor when someone is brought in front of them, that person is 'clapped in the jail' (p. 44).

Elizabeth asks John to go to Salem and denounce Abigail as a fraud. She asks her husband to tell Cheever that Abigail had told John, in Parris's house, that 'it had naught to do with witchcraft' (p. 44). Proctor says that Abigail told him this when he was alone with her and this upsets Elizabeth. John cannot go to the court at this point as he would have to admit to his affair with Abigail and so blacken his name. John regrets having confessed his affair to Elizabeth. He realises that he has probably made a mistake in doing so. His disgust at his guilt will later prove fatal in the court scene.

CHECKPOINT 11

How are John and Elizabeth affected by Abigail?

GLOSSARY

part like the sea for Israel Moses parted the Red Sea to allow the Israelites to escape from Egypt

pp. 46–51 – Mary Warren returns

① Mary returns from court and brings Elizabeth a poppet.

② Sarah Good has been arrested.

③ Proctor threatens Mary but she stands up to him.

④ There is a rumour that Elizabeth is involved in the witchcraft and she worries about Abigail's intentions.

CHECKPOINT 12

What do you notice here about Abigail?

Mary returns from the court. Proctor is annoyed that she has not been attending to her duties in the house, especially as Elizabeth is not well. Mary gives Elizabeth the gift of a doll which she has sewn whilst sitting in court. She brings news that thirty-nine women have now been arrested and that Goody Osburn will hang. Mary also says that Sarah Good has confessed to having made 'a compact with Lucifer' (p. 47) and that she had sent her spirit out and tried to choke Mary in the courtroom. John and Elizabeth do not believe her but Mary says that Sarah Good caused her to have stomach pains because she turned the old woman away when she came begging. Sarah Good claimed in court that she had not been mumbling a spell to Mary but had been saying her commandments. However, when asked to recite the commandments, she could not remember a single one. Proctor does

not seem to agree with Mary that this is 'hard proof' (p. 48). The treatment of Sarah Good is an indication of the fate that is to befall Proctor. Mary feels that 'it's God's work we do' (p. 49) but Proctor points out that hanging old women is 'strange work for a Christian girl' (p. 48). He loses his temper and threatens to whip Mary, but she stops him by saying that she saved Elizabeth's life in court that day. Elizabeth has been accused but Mary will not say by whom. Mary tells Proctor that he must 'speak civilly' (p. 49) to her and that she will not be ordered around by him.

A dangerous change in Mary Warren

Mary Warren is starting to lose her shyness as she begins to feel that she is important to the court. She has caught the communal hysteria and is embroidering fact with fantasy when she talks of Sarah Good. For the first time in her life Mary finds that adults will listen to her and treat her with respect. This goes to her head.

Behind her new-found bravery Mary is still terrified of Abigail and lacks the strength to stand up to her.

Elizabeth feels sure that she will be proclaimed a witch by Abigail: 'She wants me dead' (p. 50). She asks Proctor to tell Abigail that he no longer feels anything for the girl and he reluctantly agrees.

> **CHECKPOINT 13**
> What terrible idea does Elizabeth recognise here?

pp. 52–58 – Hale and the Proctors

1 Hale has come to test the Proctors.

2 Proctor tells Hale about the girls' foolishness.

Reverend Hale appears in the doorway of Proctor's house. Hale is already feeling guilty about his involvement in the court's proceedings. He says that he is visiting houses in the area in order to form an opinion of the people who are accused. He has just come from Rebecca Nurse's house as she has been mentioned in the court,

> **GLOSSARY**
> **Lucifer** the devil. The name means 'bringer of light' and Lucifer was the brightest angel in Heaven before he was cast out for being too proud

DID YOU KNOW?

Puritans did not believe in decoration or ornament – especially in church. Parris is clearly interested in his own image.

though she has not been charged as yet. (The Putnams are responsible for the accusations against Rebecca Nurse.)

Hale asks Proctor some questions 'as to the Christian character of this house' (p. 53). He asks why Mr Parris's records show that Proctor has been to church only twenty-six times in seven months and Proctor replies that he does not hold himself accountable to Parris. Proctor adds that Parris kept asking the congregation for golden candlesticks until he had them. Hale presses John as to why only two of his three boys had been baptised and Proctor says that he did not want Parris to lay his hands on his son. He has, however, helped with carpentry on the church and this impresses Hale.

Elizabeth and John are then asked if they know their commandments, but John cannot remember them all. He forgets the sin of adultery, and has to be reminded of it by Elizabeth. Hale sees this as a 'crack in a fortress' of theology (p. 55).

CHECKPOINT 14

How does Proctor's information affect Hale?

The existence of witchcraft is questioned

Elizabeth is anxious about her own safety, as she is suspected of practising witchcraft. She forces John to tell Hale, 'I know the children's sickness had naught to do with witchcraft' but that they were 'startled' at being caught dancing in the woods (p. 56). Hale's own beliefs are shaken by what Proctor tells him about the girls. He is forced to face up to the fact that he has been taken in by them.

Proctor agrees to make this statement in court. Hale then asks the Proctors whether they believe in witches. John says that he will not contradict the Bible, but Elizabeth insists otherwise: 'If you think that I am one, then I say there are none' (p. 57). Hale tells them to baptise their third child, go to church each Sunday and to appear solemn in their manner. This reminds us of the strict religious code of the time. It is now clear that Hale himself believes in witches, but he is uncertain as to the nature of the recent accusations.

Just before Giles Corey enters, Hale seems to have been fully convinced that the Proctors are telling that truth about the girls' testimony. He is prevented from acting upon this by the news that Corey brings.

pp. 58–66 – Elizabeth is arrested

1 More women have been arrested.

2 Hale still believes the girls.

3 Cheever has a warrant for Elizabeth's arrest.

4 A 'poppet' is found with a needle stuck inside it.

5 Elizabeth is arrested.

Giles Corey and Francis Nurse enter and Giles says that both his wife and Rebecca Nurse have been arrested. Giles Corey's earlier accusations about his wife reading strange books has not helped her. People such as Mrs Putnam and Walcott are clearly using the court proceedings to carry out their private revenge upon their neighbours. Rebecca has been charged with 'the marvellous and supernatural murder of Goody Putnam's babies' (p. 58). Hale assures Nurse that

EXAMINER'S SECRET

At this stage in the play, look at the way in which Abigail and the girls have fooled most of the town's adults. This will help you to comment on Abigail's character.

GLOSSARY
poppet a rag doll

the justice of the court will ensure that Rebecca is freed. Hale still believes that he has seen proof of witchcraft in the courtroom. Corey's wife has been charged by Walcott, Susanna's father. Walcott has had a dispute with Martha Corey over a pig he had bought from her.

CHECKPOINT 15

Why do the men come to Proctor for help?

Cheever and Herrick enter; they are on court business. Cheever has a warrant for the arrest of Elizabeth Proctor. He has also been instructed to search the house for poppets. He sees one on the mantelpiece; it is Mary's and she is sent for.

The truth

The true events surrounding the poppet are:

- Mary Warren was sewing a poppet in court to pass the time as she was bored.

- She stuck the needle in the poppet to keep it safe.

- Abigail saw Mary do this.

- During dinner at Parris's house, Abigail fell to the floor screaming and a needle was found stuck two inches into the flesh of her belly.

- When the poppet is examined by Cheever it is found to have a needle stuck in it.

It is clear to the reader that Abigail has watched Mary stick the needle in the poppet and has later stabbed herself with a needle, knowing that by this time the poppet will be in Elizabeth Proctor's house. She wants to revenge herself upon Elizabeth.

CHECKPOINT 16

What aspect of Hale's character is shown here?

Mary admits to putting the needle in the doll herself and says 'Ask Abby, Abby sat beside me when I made it.' but Parris suspects that this might not be her 'natural memory' (p. 62). Proctor rips the warrant and accuses Hale of being like Pontius Pilate. He says that the warrant is simply 'vengeance' (p. 63). When Herrick chains Elizabeth, Proctor promises to 'pay' him for it (p. 64). Giles tells Hale to act, as Hale knows this is all fraud, but Hale says that there must be some cause for all the accusations.

Proctor is left alone with Mary and he tells her that she must admit to the court how the poppet came to be in his house with a needle stuck in it. Mary is frightened and says that she cannot do it as Abigail would kill her and 'charge lechery' (p. 65) on Proctor. Thus Mary reveals that she knows of the affair. The Act closes with Mary weeping that she cannot do what Proctor has asked her. The power that Abigail has over the girls is clearly shown in Mary's terror at the prospect of having to denounce Abigail in court.

DID YOU KNOW?

The use of dolls to cast spells on people was thought to be a method used by witches. It is also connected with the voodoo that Tituba claims to practise.

Confusion

At this point in the play there is a great deal of confusion. The only characters who realise what is actually happening are the Proctors and Abigail. This is highly ironic as Abigail is now thinking of a way to hurt Elizabeth. The other characters are involved in different ways and for different reasons but confusion reigns:

- Hale is confused at the Proctors' seemingly good nature and still believes the girls are telling the truth.

- The Putnams are exploiting the confusion in order to settle old scores.

- The judges firmly believe in the testimony of the girls and have allowed themselves to be tricked.

- The townsfolk are divided between wanting to stop the arrests and fearing the power of the court and the church.

- Mary Warren is so confused as to believe she is actually doing good work in the court.

Now take a break!

WHO SAYS ...?

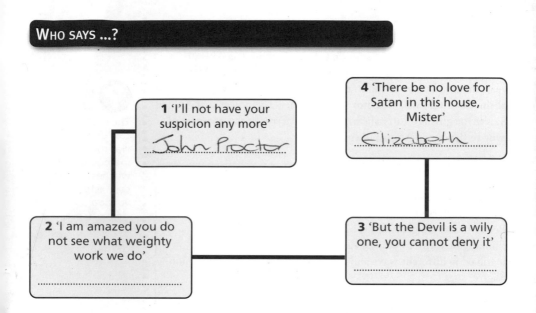

1 'I'll not have your suspicion any more'

John Proctor

4 'There be no love for Satan in this house, Mister'

Elizabeth

2 'I am amazed you do not see what weighty work we do'

3 'But the Devil is a wily one, you cannot deny it'

ABOUT WHOM?

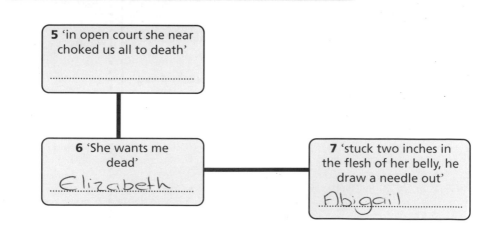

5 'in open court she near choked us all to death'

6 'She wants me dead'

Elizabeth

7 'stuck two inches in the flesh of her belly, he draw a needle out'

Abigail

Check your answers on p. 72.

pp. 67–79 – Proctor brings new evidence

1. Giles pleads for his wife.
2. Mary says the girls are all pretending.
3. Hale begins to change his mind.
4. Putnam continues to cause trouble.

The Act opens in the meeting-house vestry. The meeting house is now being used as the General Court. Judge Hathorne can be heard questioning Martha Corey, who denies hurting the children. Giles Corey cries out that 'Thomas Putnam is reaching out for land!' (p. 67). Giles is removed from the court and brought into the vestry by Herrick. He is followed by Hale, Deputy-Governor Danforth and Hathorne. Giles thinks that his wife has been arrested because he said she read strange books.

Hale tries to intercede on behalf of Giles and Francis Nurse. Francis says that he and Giles have evidence that 'the girls are frauds' (p. 70). Hathorne wants the two men arrested for contempt of court but Danforth begins to listen to them, first reminding them just how important he is.

CHECKPOINT 17

What do you see of Hathorne's character in the opening of Act III?

Proctor enters with Mary Warren, who cannot bring herself to look at anyone in the room. She has not been in court for a week, claiming that she was sick. Giles Corey says that 'She has been strivin' with her soul all week' (p. 70) and that she has now come to tell the truth. Parris warns Danforth to beware Proctor, but Hale is eager for this new evidence to be heard. Proctor tells Danforth that Mary Warren 'never saw no spirits' (p. 71) and tries to hand him a deposition stating this. Danforth will not accept the deposition. Mary says that 'It were pretence' (p. 71) from the start.

However, Parris and Hathorne seem fearful of the court being overturned and try to turn Proctor's defence of his wife and the other accused into an attack upon the court. Proctor's intentions are brought into question when Cheever points out that he tore up the court's warrant. Danforth asks Proctor if he has seen the Devil. Proctor replies that he is a Christian, but Parris reminds Danforth of Proctor's poor attendance at church. Cheever adds that John Proctor ploughs on Sundays, but Hale says this is no evidence to condemn a man with. Proctor claims once again that Mary will denounce the other girls as liars.

Elizabeth is pregnant and so will be allowed to live until she has had the child, but only if John withdraws his charge against the girls. Danforth decides to read Proctor's deposition and finds that ninety-one people have stated that they never saw Elizabeth, Martha or Rebecca having dealings with the Devil. Parris insists that these people should be summoned, but Francis Nurse replies angrily that he has given his word that 'no harm would come to them for signing this' (p. 75). Danforth is impressed with the list of names but he still continues with his narrow line of thinking. Danforth then reads Giles Corey's deposition and is impressed with his use of legal terms. Giles says that is because he has been in court thirty-three times.

As a result of Giles's deposition, Putnam is sent for. Putnam is then accused of persuading his daughter 'to cry witchery upon George Jacobs' (p. 77), so that Jacobs would be executed and then Putnam could buy his property cheaply. Putnam is greedy for land and is prepared to have innocent people killed so that he can increase his own wealth. Only Putnam has the money to buy George Jacobs's land

DID YOU KNOW?

There are clear parallels here with the McCarthy era, where people joined in with mass hysteria to blacken their rivals and so profit themselves.

but the judges fail to see the connection. Giles declares more 'proof': 'The day his daughter cried out on Jacobs, he said she'd given him a fair gift of land' (p. 77). Giles will not give the name of the man who told him this, for fear that the informant will go to jail. Parris and Hathorne refuse to accept the notion of such information being given in confidence. Hale tries to persuade Danforth that keeping the name secret is a natural thing to do as many people are afraid of the court. Giles tries to attack Putnam and threatens to cut his throat; John stops him and calms him down. However, we sympathise with Giles's frustration: even though it is becoming clear that the court proceedings are ridiculous, the judges cannot back down.

> **CHECKPOINT 18**
>
> Why are Hathorne's actions important here?

pp. 79–96 – Mary confronts the girls

1 **Mary gives her evidence.**

2 **The girls are questioned.**

3 **Proctor accuses Abigail.**

4 **Elizabeth's lie condemns her husband.**

5 **The girls distract the court.**

6 **Mary falls back under Abigail's spell.**

Danforth reads Mary's deposition and orders Parris to be silent when he tries to interrupt. The girls are sent for. Danforth asks Mary about Proctor: 'Has he threatened you?' (p. 81). Mary says he has not and admits to having lied in court, even when she knew people would be executed on her evidence. At this point Susanna Walcott, Mercy Lewis, Betty Parris and Abigail are brought in.

Abigail is asked whether there is any truth in Mary's statement; she says there is not. When Abigail is questioned, she keeps to her lie about the poppet very carefully. John says that his wife never kept poppets and that Mary Warren has also said so. Danforth warns Proctor, 'You are charging Abigail Williams with a marvellous cool plot to murder' (p. 84), but Proctor stands firm.

Proctor tells Danforth that the girls were caught dancing in the woods and Danforth begins to question Parris about this. Parris is desperate to keep his family out of the revelations about the dancing in the forest, but he cannot. He is not interested in justice, merely in saving his own name. Danforth is clearly becoming more and more suspicious of Parris as he finds out about the girls' antics in the forest but he fails to act.

CHECKPOINT 19

Where does Abigail nearly go too far?

Hathorne begins to question Mary and asks her to pretend to faint now as she claims to have done before. Mary cannot, but still maintains that she never saw any spirits. She says that it was all 'only sport in the beginning' (p. 86) but that when the girls began to be believed she was carried along with them. Abigail denies this vigorously but makes the mistake of saying 'Let *you* beware, Mr Danforth' (p. 87). Abigail realises her error and pretends to be affected by a cold wind. This idea of a cold wind blowing as the Devil appears is mentioned by Hale in Act I and Abigail exploits it here to make her story more believable. Proctor attacks Abigail and tells the court: 'I have known her, sir' (p. 88). He says that the affair is the reason why Abigail has had Elizabeth charged. Danforth sends for Elizabeth and orders no one to speak to her and Proctor to turn his back. John tells Danforth that Elizabeth knew of the affair and that it was the reason that his wife put Abigail out of the house.

Elizabeth is brought into the room. She tries to protect her husband and so denies all knowledge of the affair between John and Abigail. It is **ironic** that she ends up condemning him as a liar and making Abigail seem believable once more. She realises too late that she should have told the truth and she is led away. Hale still believes Proctor as he feels that Elizabeth's statement 'is a natural lie to tell' (p. 91).

The 'yellow bird' episode

At this point Abigail screams and claims that there is a bird on the beam above and that it is attempting to attack her. She speaks to the bird as though it is or has been sent by Mary. When Mary tries to stop her, Abigail repeats Mary's words, 'Abby, you mustn't!' (p. 93). Abigail's power is once more evident as she goes on to control the girls psychologically just as much as she did physically in Act I. The other girls soon join Abigail in mimicking Mary.

The girls flee from the yellow bird that they say is attacking. This so frightens Mary that she runs to the group of girls and is immediately comforted by them. Proctor's attempts to persuade the court that the girls are merely pretending are thwarted when Mary cries out 'You're the Devil's man!' (p. 95). She further claims that Proctor tried to make her sign the Devil's book. Proctor is arrested and accused of being 'combined with anti-Christ' (p. 96). Hale denounces the court and leaves with Danforth angrily calling after him.

CHECKPOINT 20

Why does Abigail pretend to be attacked once again?

GLOSSARY

anti-Christ the opposite to Christ, i.e. the Devil

Now take a break!

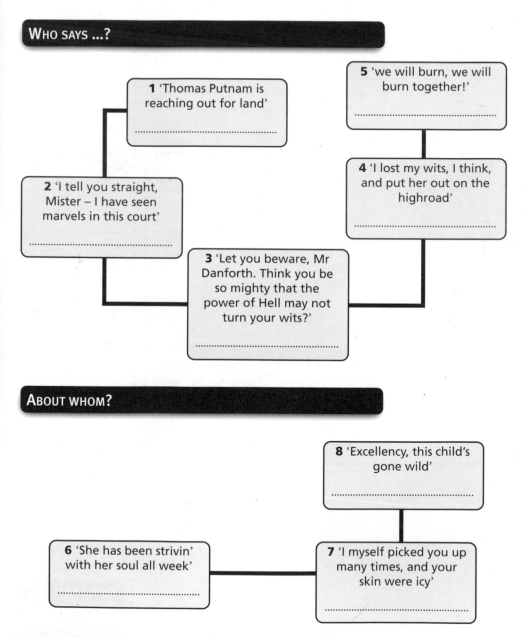

WHO SAYS ...?

1 'Thomas Putnam is reaching out for land'

....

2 'I tell you straight, Mister – I have seen marvels in this court'

....

3 'Let you beware, Mr Danforth. Think you be so mighty that the power of Hell may not turn your wits?'

....

5 'we will burn, we will burn together!'

....

4 'I lost my wits, I think, and put her out on the highroad'

....

ABOUT WHOM?

8 'Excellency, this child's gone wild'

....

6 'She has been strivin' with her soul all week'

....

7 'I myself picked you up many times, and your skin were icy'

....

Check your answers on p. 72.

pp. 97–116 – Day of execution

① Sarah Good and Tituba are executed.

② Abigail has vanished.

③ Proctor faces a difficult choice.

④ Proctor is hanged.

Those who confess to witchcraft are released, but have to live with the reputation of having been witches; those who refuse to confess are hanged. It is the day of execution for Sarah Good and Tituba. In a cell in Salem jail later that autumn, they spend their time talking about flying off to Barbados with the Devil. As the women are taken away, Danforth and Hathorne arrive with Cheever. Hale is somewhere in the prison and Parris has been spending a great deal of time recently praying with the prisoners. Hale is trying to persuade several of the prisoners to confess their witchcraft and so save their lives. We see in this Act that Hale has finally faced up to his part in the arrests and convictions, declaring 'There is bloood on my head!' (p. 105).

Parris announces that Abigail vanished three days ago with Mercy Lewis. Abigail has broken into Parris's strongbox and stolen all his money. Parris thinks she has fled because she has heard the rumour that the nearby town of Andover threw out the court when it tried to examine for witchhcraft. Parris feels similarly uneasy and warns of a 'riot' in Salem (p. 101). Few people came to hear Proctor's excommunication and Parris feels this is a warning of discontent in the town. He says that hanging Rebecca Nurse and John Proctor is very different from hanging some of the simple, poor people executed so far. Thus we see a double standard operating with regard to the executions. Only now that reputable people are to be executed is any great concern shown. In addition, the minister is fearful for his own safety should Proctor hang.

Despite Parris's protestations, Danforth refuses to grant Proctor a stay of execution. Danforth is out to save himself. His twisted logic has little to do with justice. Look at the way he conducts himself in the last section of the play. Parris says he will pray with Proctor until

> **CHECKPOINT 21**
>
> How has Hale changed from his behaviour in Act 1?

> **CHECKPOINT 22**
>
> Why do you think Abigail has disappeared?

dawn. Danforth has had twelve people hanged so far and says he cannot pardon the remaining prisoners as it would not be just. They speak of Proctor, who is chained in his cell. Danforth wonders if seeing Elizabeth might cause him to change his mind and confess. Elizabeth is brought in and Danforth and Hale try to talk her into speaking to John with a view to asking him to confess. She knows him well and says, 'I promise nothing. Let me speak with him' (p. 106). Proctor is brought in, chained, dirty and looking much older.

CHECKPOINT 23

What part of the confession does Proctor find impossible?

Husband and wife are left alone. John asks after his sons and he is told that they are being looked after by Rebecca Samuel. John has been tortured and knows that he is soon to be executed. Giles Corey has been put to death. He would not answer the accusations one way or the other and so was pressed to death.

Proctor says that he has reached a decision and will confess. He feels less sure of this when Elizabeth tells him that Martha Corey has not confessed and will hang in the morning. Elizabeth has come to terms with her husband's affair with Abigail and thinks that it was partly her fault for being a 'cold wife' (p. 109).

Hathorne enters and asks Proctor if he has changed his mind. John simply replies 'I want my life' (p. 110). Danforth and Cheever arrive and Danforth wants John to sign a confession. He asks why it must be written and is told that it will be displayed on the door of the church as an example to others.

He confesses to

- Having seen the Devil
- Agreeing to do the Devil's work on earth

During his confession, Rebecca Nurse is brought in. She is given the chance to confess and says she will not confess to a lie: 'how may I damn myself? I cannot, I cannot' (p. 112). It is almost certainly Rebecca Nurse that makes Proctor realise that it is wrong to tell such a lie.

When John is asked if he ever saw Rebecca Nurse with the Devil, he says he did not. He gives the same answer when asked about several other people and Danforth realises that Proctor is not really confessing at all. He will confess to his own sins, but is not prepared to tarnish anyone else's name.

The decision to die

When told he must sign his confession, Proctor at first refuses, then he signs it and snatches it away from Danforth. Proctor says that he has signed the confession, they have seen him sign it and that they have no need to take the paper away with them. His sense of honour means that he does not want his friends and family to know he has been weak on the day when others will have been hanged. Proctor tears the confession and seals his fate. Proctor helps Rebecca to walk to the scaffold. Parris and Hale try one last time to get Elizabeth to reason with her husband. She refuses and, from the cell window, watches him die, saying finally; 'He have his goodness now. God forbid I take it from him!' (p. 116)

CHECKPOINT 24

Why does Rebecca Nurse have such an impact on Proctor?

 CHECK THE NET

The original court records are being published on the web in stages. Visit the project at **www.iath.virginia. edu/salem/test/ intro.html**

p. 117 – Echoes down the corridor

After the events of this play and the executions

- Parris was voted out of office and never heard of again.

- Abigail is said to have turned up as a prostitute in Boston.

- Twenty years after the executions, surviving victims were awarded compensation.

- Some people still refused to admit their guilt.

- The excommunications were overturned in 1712.

- Farms belonging to the victims remained unoccupied for up to a hundred years.

This afterword adds to the authenticity of the drama. In the manner of a true-crime story we are given information about subsequent events and repercussions and this helps to remind us that the play is based upon real events which happened to real people.

? DID YOU KNOW?

The real John Proctor was an innkeeper, not a farmer.

WHO SAYS ...?

1 'It is a providence. Reverend Hale has returned to bring Rebecca Nurse to God'

....

2 'Thirty-one pound is gone. I am penniless'

Rev Paris

5 'If it is a lie I will not accept it!'

.... *Danforth* ....

4 'I cannot mount the gibbet like a saint'

.... *John Proctor* ....

3 'I think that be the Devil's argument'

....

ABOUT WHOM?

6 'A pair of bluebirds wingin' southerly, the two of us!'

....

7 'I should not be surprised he have been preaching in Andover lately'

....

8 'This woman never thought she done the Devil's work'

Rebecca Nurse

Check your answers on p. 72.

PART THREE

COMMENTARY

THEMES

PURIFICATION

A crucible is a container in which metals and other materials are heated so as to separate the pure metals from waste and impurities. The crucible in the title is a **metaphor** for the town of Salem and the period of the witch-hunt hysteria. In this 'fire', some victims survive the temptations and fears and emerge as better and stronger people.

TYRANNY

The Crucible shows a group of people reacting within a state of tyranny, in this case tyranny exerted by religious bigots, who manipulate a situation for their own purposes and choose to misinterpret events for their own ends. Finally, the situation and the events develop their own momentum and veer out of control.

BIGOTRY

Throughout the events in Salem we see the effects of religious zeal, fear of heresy, intolerance and superstition. Reverend Hale is so proud of his knowledge of witchcraft that he is quick to accept the girls' confessions as proof of this skill. Others are more than willing to accept supernatural reasons or 'unnatural causes' (p. 7) for their problems. There is so much insecurity in the young colony that anyone who questions the authorities, either religious or state, is seen to be launching an attack on the whole foundations of society.

CONFLICT

The conflict between the security of the community and 'individual freedom' (p. 5) is one theme which runs through the play. Salem was a community which felt under siege, threatened by the dangers of the wilderness, the possible corrupting influences of other Christian sects, and a genuine fear of the Devil. The play has obvious parallels with the McCarthy investigations, which were proceeding when it was first produced. *The Crucible* has been seen as a simple **allegory** of the

CHECK THE BOOK

Look at two novels which deal with the seventeenth-century witch-hunts – this time in Lancashire: *The Lancashire Witches* by William Harrison Ainsworth (1848, Grafton Books, 1988), and *Mist over Pendle* by Robert Neill (Arrow, 1992).

abuse of state power by those who persecuted and denounced people who were thought to be undermining the American way of life. Just as in Salem, any who opposed McCarthy's investigations were treated as enemies of the state.

INTEGRITY

Honesty and personal integrity are important themes. The most admirable characters who retain their dignity are those who will not subscribe to lies. Rebecca Nurse and Elizabeth Proctor are shining examples: both insist on the truth, regardless of the consequences for themselves. John Proctor is finally at peace with himself when he decides to die rather than give up his good name. He is purified in the 'crucible' of the stresses and temptations he is subjected to. On the other hand, Reverend Hale (who at the end begs Proctor to lie, admit to witchcraft and save his life) is miserable, mentally tortured and morally bankrupt.

LOYALTY

Loyalty is a theme which is illustrated in the behaviour of John Proctor towards his friends. He is tempted to withdraw his charges against Abigail and her group when he is told that his wife is pregnant and is not in immediate danger of hanging, but he goes ahead to support his friends whose wives have also been accused. Elizabeth, although she has been badly hurt by her husband's affair with Abigail, is too loyal to shame him in court and denies knowledge of it. Ironically her loyalty destroys John's case against Abigail.

COURAGE

We are shown courage in the behaviour of the accused, particularly Rebecca Nurse. As she goes to be hanged she tells John to 'fear nothing!' (p. 116) as another judgement awaits them. John tells his wife to defy the authorities and to show them no tears. We hear of Giles Corey's stubborn courage in refusing to answer the charges so that his sons may inherit his farm. His last defiant words, as he was being crushed to death, were 'More weight' (p. 108).

 CHECK THE BOOK
Arthur Koestler's *Darkness at Noon*, published in 1940, takes place in an unnamed country, but one that people have identified as 1930s' Russia, under Stalin's cruel regime. An old revolutionary is encouraged to confess to crimes he did not commit, for the good of the state.

CHECK THE NET

You can see maps of Salem in 1692 at **www.iath.virginia.edu/salem/test/maps.html**

ENVY

Envy and resentment are demonstrated in the Putnams' quarrels over land and Ann Putnam's bitter feelings towards Rebecca Nurse and her healthy family. These feelings are converted to self-serving accusations of witchcraft. Abigail is envious of Elizabeth's position as John Proctor's wife and it is possible that she believes she can take her place once Elizabeth is out of the way.

STRUCTURE

ACT I

We are immediately presented with the fear of witchcraft which is beginning to spread. The first Act also gives us the background to the conflicts within the small community of Salem. We see that there are disputes over land and dissatisfaction with the minister. Many of the main characters are introduced.

 DID YOU KNOW?

The events in Salem actually took place in a number of different locations. Miller has reduced the number of locations to one per Act in order to make the drama function on stage.

ACT II

The second Act shows us the uneasy relationship between John and Elizabeth Proctor. The tension is raised by the impending danger to Elizabeth and reaches a climax in the highly charged incident of her arrest. During most of this Act there are only two or three characters present and the drama is more intimate. The focus is on John and Elizabeth but Abigail's influence is felt throughout.

ACT III

The third Act takes place in the courtroom and presents us with the life-or-death struggle between superstition and reason. Hopes are raised and dashed. A crucial point in the drama is reached when John confesses to his adultery. We feel that this should finally destroy Abigail's credibility, but the tables are turned when Elizabeth's misplaced loyalty destroys his case. Mary Warren's attempt to recant is defeated by the force of Abigail's personality (and that of her followers), and she denounces John Proctor who is arrested.

Act I	Act II	Act III	Act IV
Reverend Parris's house	Proctor's house	Courtroom	Jail
John quarrels with Parris. Rejects Abigail's advances	John defends himself to Elizabeth and to Hale. Struggles against Elizabeth's arrest, gets Mary to recant	John defends Elizabeth and neighbours' wives, confesses to adultery, encourages Mary to recant and is arrested	John confesses, to live and look after his children, but tears up the confession and goes to die rather than besmirch his good name
Elizabeth is spoken of as 'cold' by Abigail	Elizabeth is cool towards John, satisfies Hale as to her character but is arrested on Abigail's word	We hear Elizabeth is pregnant and will not hang immediately. She is brought in to support John's confession of adultery but she will not shame him publicly	Elizabeth allows John to make up his own mind about confessing. She supports him and refuses to try to influence him when he chooses death
Reverend Hale arrives full of pride in his knowledge. He soon extracts 'confessions'	Hale has doubts about the witch-hunt and makes his own enquiries, visits the Proctors and is shocked by Elizabeth's arrest	Hale tries to intercede for the accused, finally denounces the court and leaves	Hale is a broken man, encouraging people to deny their faith to save their lives
Abigail is in trouble through dancing in the woods and begins to denounce people. She shows desire for John Proctor and hatred for Elizabeth	We hear Abigail is the star witness in the witch trials. She has denounced Elizabeth	Abigail leads the girls in court. She defies John Proctor and even Danforth. She defeats Mary Warren	We hear that Abigail has absconded with Reverend Parris's money

CHECK THE NET

For a recreation of Salem in 1692 visit:
fisher.lib.virginia. edu/projects/ salem/

ACT IV

The final Act allows us to see John Proctor grow into a noble and heroic character who chooses to die rather than deny himself and his good name. It is **ironic** that the once-proud Hale is reduced to the stage where he is begging John to lie to avoid being hanged. There is a dramatic twist when John confesses and then recants. In this Act the relationship between John and Elizabeth is seen to have grown stronger than ever.

CHARACTERS

JOHN PROCTOR

Decent
Forthright
Courageous

John Proctor is a farmer with a down-to-earth, 'steady manner' (p. 16). He tries to be a decent husband and citizen, is 'respected and even feared in Salem' (p. 16) but, as we soon discover, he is no saint. He has had a sexual relationship with Abigail Williams when she was a servant at the farm. He does not attend church as often as he should, and he is not thoroughly familiar with scripture, as is shown when he cannot easily recite the Ten Commandments.

Although he speaks his mind and stands up to Parris, he has no wish to be a martyr and he is careful about what he says when he senses real danger. He does show courage and boldness in his opposition to Parris and Putnam and he fiercely resists the arrest of his wife.

Although he usually shows 'a quiet confidence' (p. 16), Proctor is cautious when it comes to denouncing Abigail, particularly when his wife, claiming to be pregnant, is not in immediate danger. However, he feels he owes it to his friends, who have been accused, to expose Abigail as a liar.

He works hard to build a defence for those accused and manages to persuade Mary Warren to tell the truth, but this success is short-lived. As a last resort, he suffers the public shame of confessing to his adultery with Abigail, to no avail.

In prison, he eventually confesses so that he can live and care for his family, but finally he decides to die rather than lose his good name by admitting to witchcraft and he will not sign the paper. He does this for the sake of his children's future reputation and because of the example of Elizabeth and others who have refused to confess. He will not deny himself. He has doubted his ability to be a good man so far, but with Elizabeth's example and support he realises he can be true to himself and accept death.

ELIZABETH PROCTOR

We hear from Abigail Williams that Elizabeth Proctor is a cold woman. John Proctor himself tells Elizabeth that her justice 'would freeze beer!' (p. 46), when they are talking about his adultery with Abigail. She seems to do her best to forgive John but she has been badly hurt and she suspects his motives when he is unwilling to denounce Abigail as a liar.

Elizabeth is confident before Reverend Hale. She knows she has observed her religious duties and that 'she keeps an upright way' (p. 57). She is honest and open about Mary's doll when she is arrested and she bravely keeps up a dignified appearance as she is taken.

Honest
Open
Devout
Dignified

Elizabeth will not confess to witchcraft: 'If you think that I am one, then I say there are none' (p. 57). To confess to witchcraft would be a denial of her faith. Truthfulness is so important to her that John Proctor asks the court to verify with her his confession of adultery. He is confident that 'That woman will never lie' (p. 74). Elizabeth's love for her husband proves to be stronger than her love of truth and she will not support the story in court and destroy his reputation. John's case against Abigail collapses.

In Act IV we see that Elizabeth has truly forgiven John and has come to realise some of her own failings. If she had been more loving and confident in their relationship, he might not have fallen into temptation.

In the end Elizabeth shows great courage as she refuses to influence her husband's decision, saying, 'Do as you will, do as you will!' (p. 111). She loves him dearly but knows that he must do what is right for himself, even if it means bringing about his own death.

Scholarly
Confident
Well-meaning
Weak

REVEREND JOHN HALE

At the beginning of the play, Reverend Hale is a confident, well-meaning 'intellectual' (p. 26) who is proud of his knowledge and expertise. He believes he holds the answers to any questions or fears concerning witchcraft which may be troubling the simple people of Salem.

He quickly takes the opportunity to show off his skills by exhorting Tituba and the girls to confess and denounce others to save themselves. He is delighted with his success, crying, 'Glory to God! It is broken, they are free!' (p. 39)

By Act II we are told *'He is different now'* (p. 52): he is less secure in his beliefs or in his enthusiasm for the proceedings in Salem. He has begun to make his own enquiries about the people who have been named, which suggests he is uneasy. He visits the Proctors' house discreetly at night and asks questions in a calm and methodical way. We feel he is genuinely seeking the truth: he says to Elizabeth that he is seeking out 'godly wisdom' (p. 56). He is critical of John Proctor's poor record of attendance at church and finds that John has difficulty in remembering the Ten Commandments. However, he is impressed by Elizabeth's declaration of her strong Christain faith.

Hale is taken aback when Elizabeth is arrested but tries to assure the Proctors that the court will be just and fair. He promises to speak up for Elizabeth. He is obviously alarmed by these developments and wonders aloud if they are due to the 'thundering wrath' of God (p. 65), punishing Salem for some great sin.

In court Hale speaks in defence of the Proctors and their friends. He is very troubled by the death warrants he has had to sign. He supports John's case against Abigail and reveals that he has always doubted her truthfulness. When John is arrested he cries out 'I denounce these proceedings!' (p. 96) and storms out of the court.

In Act IV, Hale tries to undo some of the harm he has helped to bring about by encouraging those condemned to death to confess and so save their lives. They will not do this and thus they show that they are truer to their faith than he is.

Although Hale has tried to do what he believes to be right and he has been able to admit his mistakes, he is a weak man. He is prepared to give up his principles to appease the witch-hunters and he lacks the courage of the victims.

ABIGAIL WILLIAMS

As a child, Abigail saw her parents slaughtered by Indians. Taken into service, she was seduced by her employer, John Proctor, jilted, then thrown out of the house when the affair was discovered. So Abigail, a strong-minded young woman – she describes herself as 'A wild thing' (p. 18) – has an axe to grind. She is determined and scheming, and will sacrifice anyone to gain her own advantage or save her own skin. She has been involved in 'mischief' (p. 17) in the forest with Tituba and the other girls. She is a very sensual person and still has a strong physical *concentrated desire* for John (p. 17). We can believe that she would like to take Elizabeth's place.

A victim
Sensual
Unscrupulous
Determined

In court, Abigail skilfully defends herself and turns suspicion on others. It seems to matter little to her that she is sending people to their deaths. She enjoys her power and feels secure enough at one point to threaten Judge Danforth. Her court performances are very convincing and at times she seems to be in a genuine trance.

Abigail ruthlessly controls the other girls from the start of the play; and this power is demonstrated most effectively in her defeat of Mary Warren's retraction. She is only completely discredited when we hear that she has run off with her uncle's savings, but this is too late to stop the train of events she has helped to set in motion.

MARY WARREN

Although the Proctors' servant, Mary Warren is involved with Abigail in denouncing innocent people, but she does not do so from malicious motives. She is a timid and excitable girl and is easily dominated by Abigail.

Gullible
Timid
Excitable

Mary is flattered by the attention she receives as an important witness in court, what she describes as 'weighty work' (p. 48). She tries to assert her new-found dignity at home: 'I'll not be ordered to bed no more, Mr Proctor!' (p. 49). However, she is horrified by the death sentences which are passed and is '*bewildered*' (p. 62) and upset by her involvement in Abigail's plot against Elizabeth Proctor, when her doll is used.

Under pressure from John, Mary agrees to expose the whole business as a 'pretence' (p. 85) but she is too weak to withstand Abigail's assault in court and she turns on John, crying out: 'You're the Devil's man!' (p. 95). This accusation results in his arrest.

REVEREND SAMUEL PARRIS

A former merchant in the West Indies, Parris is a pompous, vain man who is unpopular with many of his congregation. Some consider him to be greedy and ambitious and others do not like his sermons, which concentrate on 'hellfire and bloody damnation' (p. 23). He believes that people are plotting against him – 'why am I persecuted here?' (p. 24) – and he is anxious to avoid any hint of scandal connected with his house. After the trials he is appalled by the executions and begs to have them delayed.

THOMAS AND ANN PUTNAM

Putnam is a wealthy farmer who is greedy for more land. Giles Corey suggests in court that Putnam will benefit from the execution of his neighbours as he is the only man with money enough to buy their farms. We learn that he is a man 'with many grievances' (p. 11). Miller tells us that the Putnam family have been involved in several disputes with their neighbours, particularly the Nurse family. Putnam was responsible for 'many accusations' (p. 11).

Mrs Putnam, Thomas's wife, is a bitter woman who has lost seven children at birth. She looks for someone or something to blame and is more than willing to believe that 'the Devil's touch' (p. 10) is responsible. She is resentful of Rebecca Nurse who has a large family.

Bitter
Greedy

REBECCA AND FRANCIS NURSE

Rebecca Nurse has a reputation for good works and Christian charity which reaches beyond Salem: she is 'the very brick and mortar of the church' (p. 58). She encourages the arguing factions to 'make your

Charitable
Peaceful

peace' (p. 25) and she calms the hysterical Betty by her mere presence. Rebecca suggests that 'good prayer' (p. 22) may be an answer to their fears about witchcraft. She does not care for Parris's hellfire sermons and she expresses doubts about the calling in of Reverend Hale.

Towards the end, under sentence of death, she is a calm, almost saintly example to the others, particularly John Proctor, who accompanies her to the scaffold.

Francis is the faithful husband of Rebecca Nurse. He and Giles Corey join with John Proctor in attempting to clear their wives of charges against them.

TITUBA

Tituba is Parris's black slave, whom he brought back to America from Barbados. Tituba appears to know about voodoo ritual – an amalgam of Christianity and African religious rites – when she admits 'I give she chicken blood!' (p. 36). Because her blackness makes her physically different, the local community have perhaps endowed her with a mystique she does not truly possess. She has been encouraged by the girls to carry out spells and other rituals in the forest. Ann Proctor sends her daughter to her to find out who killed her babies because she 'knows how to speak to the dead' (p. 12). When challenged, Tituba is terrified and will confess to anything. We see her in jail with Sarah Good in Act IV, where she has pathetic illusions about flying to Barbados with the Devil.

• Mysterious
• Exotic

BETTY

Betty is the Reverend Parris's ten-year-old daughter. Her strange illness triggers the fears of witchcraft in Salem. She is under Abigail's influence and takes part in the court proceedings.

MERCY LEWIS AND SUSANNA WALCOT

Mercy is the Putnams' servant, a sly and vindictive member of Abigail's group. She denounces people and is with Abigail and the others in court. After the trials we hear that she has run away with Abigail.

Susanna is a young member of Abigail's group. She is a nervous and frightened girl.

GILES CORY

Giles is an elderly, argumentative but honest farmer. His hobby is taking people to court. He quarrels with Thomas Putnam over a piece of land. Foolishly he mentions his wife's fondness for reading and puts her under suspicion. He knows the law well and he refuses to answer the charge of witchcraft so that his sons may inherit his land. Had he denied the charge, he would have been hanged and his land would have been forfeited. He is pressed to death under large stones.

CHECK THE NET
A detailed account of the real characters can be read at **www.ogram.org**

JUDGE HATHORNE

Hathorne is a cold, unbending judge who believes that anyone protesting against the sentences or trying to defend the accused must be in league with them and against the administration of the law.

DEPUTY-GOVERNOR DANFORTH

Danforth is more human than Hathorne and he is prepared to listen to new evidence, such as Mary Warren's retraction. However, he is very firm in his defence of the court and its proceedings.

MARSHAL HERRICK

Herrick is a court officer. He is a kindly man and is obviously unhappy about arresting people like Elizabeth Proctor and keeping them in jail.

EZEKIEL CHEEVER

Cheever is clerk of the court and serves the warrant for Elizabeth's arrest. He is a humourless and petty man.

SARAH GOOD

Sarah is a poor, confused, old woman who confesses to witchcraft and shares a cell with Tituba. They talk together about going to Barbados with the Devil.

LANGUAGE AND STYLE

The language spoken by the characters in the play is intended to give us the feeling of a society which is different from ours in time and manners. When he was researching the play, Miller was intrigued by the language of the court records and adapted some of the forms and usages for his dialogue. He does not use the exact form of English that the people of Salem would have recognised as this might prove too difficult for a modern audience to understand. Instead, Miller gives us a flavour of the language spoken in seventeenth-century America.

THE INFLUENCE OF LATIN

The English spoken at the time of the events in Salem was heavily influenced by Latin. Most educated people would have used Latin for written communication and many important texts were available only in Latin. In Latin, the verb usually comes at the end of the sentence, e.g. 'Up the stairs she climbed.' If you find that some of the word order in *The Crucible* is unusual it is because we have now moved away from this way of constructing sentences.

As Latin had been used by the church in order to keep the Bible from ordinary people, the Puritans of Salem rebelled against the language itself but still spoke in a way that reflected the English of their home country. Note that in Act I, when Reverend Hale wants to drive out the Devil, he chants in Latin.

Miller uses double negatives and **inverted** sentence structures in his version of this language. John Proctor says, 'I never said no such thing' (p. 25), Giles Corey tells Danforth, 'I will not give you no name' (p. 78). In Act IV, Danforth tells Elizabeth 'we come not for your life' (p. 105) when the modern version would be, 'we do not come for your life'. 'What think you, Mr Parris?' (p. 104) would be 'What do you think?'. In his autobiography *Timebends*, Miller said of the language:

> I came to love its feel, like hard burnished wood. Without planning to, I even elaborated a few of the grammatical forms myself, the double negatives especially, which occurred in the trial record much less frequently than they would in the play.

> **CHECKPOINT 25**
>
> How is the language of *The Crucible* different from the English spoken today?

Some words are used in a way that we would not use them now. Giles Corey, complaining about his wife's reading habits, says, 'It discomforts me!' (p. 33), using 'discomfort' as a verb, whereas we would say, 'It makes me uncomfortable'. John Proctor expresses amazement that Mr Hale would 'suspicion' his wife (p. 57). Modern usage would be 'suspect'.

CHRISTIANITY AND THE BIBLE

DID YOU KNOW?

The King James Bible of 1611 had a great influence on the English language.

The rhythms and the **imagery** of the language echo that of the King James's version of the Bible of 1611. The Puritans in England, forefathers of the Salem settlers, had requested a new translation of the Bible as part of their pressures for reform of the Church. It took seven years to complete and had a definite influence on style. This Authorised Version, used by Protestants for 350 years, was loved for the beauty and clarity of its English and would have been familiar to the audiences of the 1950s and still is to many today. It was only replaced by modern versions around 1960.

The forenames of the characters and others mentioned are taken from the Bible, as was the practice in Christian communities. Some of them which are not so commonly used today, such as Ezekiel, Isaac and Susanna are from the Old Testament. Others, like John, Thomas, Martha and Elizabeth, can be found in the New Testament.

A good deal of the language found in *The Crucible* has its origins in religion. As the Puritans took the Bible literally they would have thought it perfectly normal to use sayings from it in everyday speech. Reverend Hale, when he describes his period of soul-searching before he tries to persuade John Proctor to save his life by confessing, says, 'I have gone this three months like our Lord into the wilderness' (p. 105). He is comparing his experience to that of Jesus when, according to St Matthew, he was, 'led up of the Spirit into the wilderness to be tempted of the devil' (Matthew, 4: 1). In Act II, speaking of Abigail, Elizabeth Proctor says, 'where she walks the crowd will part like the sea for Israel' (p. 43), which is a reference to the parting of the Red Sea in the book of Exodus when Moses led the Israelites in their escape from Egypt. When Danforth is asked to delay the executions, he replies, 'God have not empowered me like Joshua to stop this sun from rising' (p. 104), which refers to Joshua, 10.

This is a powerful, dignified way of speaking which helps to create the impression of a different society, one which is rural and deeply religious. It is a deliberate and simple language, which is appropriate to the period in which the play is set without being too difficult for the modern audience.

Within this form of language some characters are made to be more eloquent than others. It is important that Abigail is an impressive speaker, whereas Mary Warren has to be more timid. It is not that the girls actually spoke exactly like this: it suits Miller's dramatic purpose to have the two girls speak differently from one another.

LANGUAGE IN CONTEXT

Arthur Miller uses the rhythms and patterns of speech that would have been heard in Salem at the time of the original trials. You need to remember this when writing about the play. The characters are not speaking old English or even funny English. It is simply that the English that we speak today has changed since the seventeenth century. If you need convincing of this, imagine how our speech might sound to people in four hundred years' time.

WWW. CHECK THE NET

The entire King James Bible is reproduced at **www.bartleby.com**

Now take a break!

PART FOUR

RESOURCES

HOW TO USE QUOTATIONS

One of the secrets of success in writing essays is the way you use quotations. There are five basic principles:

❶ Put inverted commas at the beginning and end of the quotation.

❷ Write the quotation exactly as it appears in the original.

❸ Do not use a quotation that repeats what you have just written.

❹ Use the quotation so that it fits into your sentence.

❺ Keep the quotation as short as possible.

EXAMINER'S SECRET

The best students use quotations fluently and incorporate them into their writing.

Quotations should be used to develop the line of thought in your essays. Your comment should not duplicate what is in your quotation. For example:

> John Proctor tells Parris and Putnam that he does not come to church because Parris preaches hellfire and bloody damnation: 'I have trouble enough without I come five mile to hear him preach only hellfire and bloody damnation' (p. 23)

Far more effective is to write:

> John Proctor says that he has not been to church as, 'I have trouble enough without I come five mile to hear him preach only hellfire and bloody damnation'

However, the most sophisticated way of using the writer's words is to embed them into your sentence:

> John Proctor tells his wife that he has 'gone tiptoe' in his own house since his affair with Abigail. (p. 45)

When you use quotations in this way, you are demonstrating the ability to use text as evidence to support your ideas – not simply including words from the original to prove you have read it.

COURSEWORK ESSAY

Set aside an hour or so at the start of your work to plan what you have to do.

- List all the points you feel are needed to cover the task. Collect page references of information and quotations that will support what you have to say. A helpful tool is the highlighter pen: this saves painstaking copying and enables you to target precisely what you want to use.

- Focus on what you consider to be the main points of the essay. Try to sum up your argument in a single sentence, which could be the closing sentence of your essay. Depending on the essay title, it could be a statement about a character: John Proctor is the hero of the play as he gives up his life rather than his good name; an opinion about a setting: The play is set in New England, a melting pot in which people's characters are put to the ultimate test; or a judgement on a theme: I think that the main theme of the play is the importance of personal honesty.

- Make a short essay plan. Use the first paragraph to introduce the argument you wish to make. In the following paragraphs develop this argument with details, examples and other possible points of view. Sum up your argument in the last paragraph. Check you have answered the question.

- Write the essay, remembering all the time the central point you are making.

- On completion, go back over what you have written to eliminate careless errors and improve expression. Read it aloud to yourself, or, if you are feeling more confident, to a relative or friend.

If you can, try to type your essay using a word processor. This will allow you to correct and improve your writing without spoiling its appearance.

 **CHECK THE NET**

Detailed background information on the play can be found at **www. webenglishteacher. com/miller.html**

SITTING THE EXAMINATION

Examination papers are carefully designed to give you the opportunity to do your best. Follow these handy hints for exam success:

BEFORE YOU START

- Make sure you know the subject of the examination so that you are properly prepared and equipped.

- You need to be comfortable and free from distractions. Inform the invigilator if anything is off-putting, e.g. a shaky desk.

- Read the instructions, or rubric, on the front of the examination paper. You should know by now what you have to do but check to reassure yourself.

- Observe the time allocation – and follow it carefully. If they recommend 60 minutes for Question 1 and 30 minutes for Question 2, it is because Question 1 carries twice as many marks.

- Consider the mark allocation. You should write a longer response for 4 marks than for 2 marks.

WRITING YOUR RESPONSES

- Use the questions to structure your response, e.g. question: 'The endings of X's poems are always particularly significant. Explain their importance with reference to two poems.' The first part of your answer will describe the ending of the first poem; the second part will look at the ending of the second poem; the third part will be an explanation of the significance of the two endings.

- Write a brief draft outline of your response.

- A typical 30-minute examination essay is probably between 400 and 600 words in length.

- Keep your writing legible and easy to read, using paragraphs to show the structure of your answers.

- Spend a couple of minutes afterwards quickly checking for obvious errors.

EXAMINER'S SECRET

You should focus clearly on the question that you have been set. All too often students simply write the same general answer no matter what the question is.

WHEN YOU HAVE FINISHED

- Don't be downhearted – if you found the examination difficult, it is probably because you really worked at the questions. Let's face it, they are not meant to be easy!

- Don't pay too much attention to what your friends have to say about the paper. Everyone's experience is different and no two people ever give the same answers.

IMPROVE YOUR GRADE

Most students can immediately make some improvement in their grade by recognising what it is that they are being asked to do. Whether you are writing a coursework essay, or are sitting the examination, all written tasks can be broken down into three simple areas:

❶ AIMS: What did the writer set out to do?

❷ MEANS: How did the writer go about doing it?

❸ SUCCESS: Was the writer successful?

1. AIMS

You should consider the author's objectives before you begin to write any lengthy answer. Arthur Miller was not simply filling up three hours of stage time with *The Crucible*. You must try to grasp what he set out to do. The plot could be summarised in a few pages, so why does the play take three hours on stage?

Though you are not necessarily studying American history, it is important that you look at the reasons behind the writing of *The Crucible* – see the section on **Setting and background**. Miller set out to achieve something quite remarkable. He had two main aims, to:

- Shed light on the events of Salem
- Draw parallels with the America of the 1950s

The play is meant to show that witch-hunts lead to hysterical

EXAMINER'S SECRET
Remember why you are writing. Do not get carried away with the story-line.

EXAMINER'S SECRET

Remember: Miller was making a political point with *The Crucible* as well as providing entertainment.

behaviour and to the persecution of innocent people for personal reasons. It is important that you realise that *The Crucible* operates therefore on two levels.

There are many playwrights who are contemporaries of Miller but whose work is no longer performed, so perhaps Miller was doing something a little different from his fellow writers. The plot of *The Crucible* is complicated; but it is the way that Miller handles the various elements of plot that makes the play interesting.

2. Means

Many students concentrate on this second area only. This results in a lengthy re-telling of the story of whatever it is they have just read. There is nothing wrong with some account of the story but if this is all you do, then you have carried out a fairly basic task. The plot of most great novels, plays and poems could be given to a class of eight-year-olds. They would then re-tell the story and draw a lovely picture. The skills shown by the eight-year-old students would not amount to much – cetainly not a high grade at GCSE!

To achieve a higher grade, you also need to consider the form and structure of *The Crucible*. Because he is writing a play, Miller does not give the audience a meticulous historical acount of the events in Salem. The play is arranged in four Acts, each Act taking place in a given location. In reality the events would have taken place in many different places and at many different times. Miller has brought together several key events for dramatic effect. Whilst the audience sees the Proctors at home, there are important events happening in Salem which are never seen. Making the audience wait is a deliberate ploy used to develop and control tension – something that great playwrights know how to do. To achieve a higher grade you would need to show that you are aware of Miller's techniques, e.g. how one part of the plot is built up to the point where a major event is about to take place and then the scene shifts to another area of plot altogether.

CHECK THE NET

There are free resources in the English sections of **www.longman. co.uk**

A major element of language use which tends to be seen by only the higher-grade students is **imagery**. Try to show how the use of imagery is responsible for creating particular impressions. For example, at the end of Act III Proctor says:

A fire, a fire is burning! I hear the boot of Lucifer, I see his filthy face! And it is my face, and yours, Danforth!   (p. 96)

He uses several words associated with hell and with the Devil. This has a much greater impact than simply referring to the Devil on one occasion. Miller is building up an image that has clear connections with aspects of our lives. We know that the people of Salem took the notion of the Devil very seriously. For Proctor to mention hell and the Devil so many times and so close together he must be trying to communicate a very strong idea.

Writers know these associations and play upon them for effect. Take the simplest idea of all – villain dressed in black; good guy dressed in white. Such basic images occur throughout the history of world literature. Good writers do not simply use such basic images. They are constantly looking out for new things to use as comparisons. To improve your grade, you need to recognise that this is how writers work and include references to it in your written answers.

EXAMINER'S SECRET

Consider how the constraints of the stage affect the story-line.

3. SUCCESS

To reach the highest level you need to consider whether the writer has been successful. For example, if you think Miller set out to create sympathetic and realistic characters, has he managed this? Do you think Miller intended us to feel some sympathy for Proctor and, if so, has he made us feel it? A higher-grade student would notice that none of the major characters is simply one-dimensional. Proctor is a good man with a guilty secret; Abigail is a devious girl who has led a hard life; Hale starts firm in his beliefs but comes to realise he has been a fool.

FURTHER ADVICE

When you come to discuss points 1–3 above, there are two basic things that you need to do:

- Decide what it is you want to say.

- Select the parts of the text that support what you want to say. (See the other **Resources** sections.)

EXAMINER'S SECRET

Don't say what you think the examiner wants you to say. Success follows when you give a personal response!

A higher-level answer will always contain the student's personal response. Do not be afraid to say **'I feel that ...'** or **'I believe...'**. You must of course have some evidence for what you suggest. There are people who still think the Earth is flat but there is pretty good evidence that it is not. Each time you make a major point you should support it, either by giving an account in your own words or by using a quotation.

The final point to bear in mind is that your own writing needs to be of a high standard. You must attempt to use the language of literary criticism when discussing a work of literature. Simply saying **'the play was good'** does not really mean anything. It does not matter whether you liked the play; the important thing to remember is that you are commenting on the effectiveness of the work. Using vocabulary beyond that you might normally use when talking to your friends is vital if you wish to come across well on paper.

Don't forget the three areas you need to cover:

❶ AIMS: What did the writer set out to do?

❷ MEANS: How did the writer go about doing it?

❸ SUCCESS: Was the writer successful?

By considering each of these three questions in detail, you should be able to improve your grade. Good luck with your writing about *The Crucible*.

SAMPLE ESSAY PLAN

What is there about the society of Salem which allows the girls' stories to be believed?

INTRODUCTION

Historical background – People had fled from England to escape religious persecution. They saw new colonies as chances to establish exemplary Christian communities. They were deeply suspicious of religious sects other than their own – Parris says: 'What, are we Quakers?' (p. 24).

PART 1 – RELIGIOUS ATTITUDES

Everyone was expected to conform to a strict code of belief. Very real belief in the existence of the Devil and his agents. Anyone who expressed an opinion which was slightly out of keeping with these deeply held beliefs was liable to be accused of heresy. Hale says, 'Theology, sir, is a fortress; no crack in a fortress may be accounted small' (p. 55). The people took a rather literal view of the Old Testament and relied upon it to explain much that was unknown: 'Thou shalt not suffer a witch to live' (Exodus, 22: 18).

PART 2 – PERSONAL DIFFERENCES

There was much jealousy between the wealthier landowners, each seeking to expand territory. There are numerous references in *The Crucible* to disputes over land boundaries and legal actions are common. There is much deep personal resentment, e.g. between

- THE PUTNAMS and PARRIS: because Parris was appointed minister instead of Putnam's brother-in-law

- PUTNAM and NURSE FAMILIES: as the Nurses had blocked the above appointment and established their own township outside Salem, thus splitting the community into factions. Mrs Putnam resents the fact that Rebecca Nurse has a healthy family whereas all of her babies died in childbirth

- ABIGAIL AND ELIZABETH PROCTOR: Abigail wants Elizabeth dead so that she can have John all to herself

PART 3 – OPPRESSIVE SOCIETY

The girls are afraid when they are caught dancing and casting spells. This fear leads them to invent stories so as to lay the blame on others. Parris is ready to see the hand of the Devil in the sickness of his daughter, rather than bring public disgrace on his house through the misbehaviour of his daughter and niece.

PART 4 – VANITY AND PRIDE

- HALE: pride in his scholarship makes Hale unwilling to accept that the girls' confessions are genuine. He is far too ready to jump to witchcraft as an explanation for all ills

EXAMINER'S SECRET

Planning an essay does take time, but it ensures that you don't repeat yourself – or leave out any of your ideas!

- DANFORTH and HATHORNE: the pride of these men makes them reluctant to consider that they could have been manipulated by a group of girls

- THE GIRLS: once the girls have started to denounce the townsfolk, it is very hard for them to retract their statements, especially when so many are ready to believe them. When Mary returns to Proctor's house (Act II) she says, 'Four judges and the King's Deputy sat to dinner with us but an hour ago' (p. 49)

- ABIGAIL: vanity leads Abigail to believe that Proctor really would take her as his wife. He even calls her 'a lump of vanity' (p. 89). She also threatens Danforth, saying, 'Let you beware, Mr Danforth. Think you be so mighty that the power of Hell may not turn your wits?' (p. 87)

CONCLUSION

The girls were believed because circumstances in Salem combined to allow some people to exact vengeance upon old enemies and others to hide their own wrongdoing. Once the executions had begun, it proved very difficult for anyone involved to accept that a terrible mistake had been made.

FURTHER QUESTIONS

Outline a plan as above and attempt to answer the following questions.

1 Discuss the changes in the relationship between John and Elizabeth Proctor in the course of the play.

2 Abigail Williams is denounced by Proctor as being 'a lump of vanity' (p. 89). How far do you agree with this comment about her?

3 Discuss the importance of religious belief in the play.

4 Many of the events in *The Crucible* occur because of the oppressive nature of the society in which people lived. Say how far you think that people's desire for individual freedom contributes to the conflict.

EXAMINER'S SECRET
Underline the key words in the question – this will help make sure that you answer it!

⑤ Discuss how far any three of the following characters can be said to remain true to his or her beliefs:

- John Proctor
- Elizabeth Proctor
- Reverend Hale
- Giles Corey
- Rebecca Nurse
- Reverend Parris

⑥ Discuss the importance of envy and greed in the play.

⑦ Comment on some of the different views about witchcraft held by characters in the play.

⑧ How does Miller create tension in the courtroom scene (Act III)?

⑨ How far do you think the themes dealt with in *The Crucible* are relevant today?

⑩ Discuss the effectiveness of Miller's use of language in creating a sense of a particular society.

DID YOU KNOW?

The community of Salem ended up persecuting innocent people even though it had been established as a refuge from the religious persecution in England.

Now take a break!

allegory a story which can be seen to have two different and parallel meanings, rather like a fable or parable. *The Crucible* can be read as an allegory of the anti-Communist investigations in the United States in the 1950s

imagery/image a picture in words. There are two obvious kinds of image, **simile** and **metaphor**

inversion/inverted a departure from normal word order. In *The Crucible* it is used to represent an older form of English, e.g., 'I know not what I have said', 'I like not the sound of it'

irony/ironic using words to convey the opposite of their literal meaning, a deliberate contrast between apparent and intended meaning; also incongruity between what might be expected and what actually occurs

metaphor a description of one thing in terms of something else, e.g., 'I have seen you looking up, burning in your loneliness', 'I have made a bell of my honour! I have rung the doom of my good name'

simile a direct comparison of one thing with another, using 'like', 'as', or 'as if', e.g., 'The crowd will part like the sea for Israel' (p. 43)

CHECKPOINT 1 Most of the girls were probably only playing a game, but it seems that Abigail and Tituba were dabbling in conjuring. Look for evidence of this in the play.

CHECKPOINT 2 Abigail has not yet seen the potential for revenge. When is the first time that we see Abigail is plotting against Elizabeth?

CHECKPOINT 3 She changes from girl to woman, the moment he enters, taking on 'a confidential, wicked air' (p. 17).

CHECKPOINT 4 Abigail was an orphan (her parents were slaughtered by Indians); she had been taken in as a servant by the Proctors. John Proctor abused Abigail's and his wife's trust by taking advantage of Abigail when she was weak.

CHECKPOINT 5 Wily old Giles likes to be involved in whatever is going on.

CHECKPOINT 6 Common-sense Rebecca has great experience with children.

CHECKPOINT 7 This petty quibble shows that Parris is a greedy and small-minded man.

CHECKPOINT 8 Mrs Putnam resents Rebecca's high moral tone.

CHECKPOINT 9 Tituba cries out these names at the end of the Act. She is simply repeating the ideas of people in the room.

CHECKPOINT 10 She realises that she will be believed if she identifies witches, and she has learned about the ways witches supposedly affect their victims.

CHECKPOINT 11 Elizabeth is jealous of Abigail; John is embarrassed that he has been alone with her.

CHECKPOINT 12 It is clear that Abigail has accused Elizabeth.

CHECKPOINT 13 She is likely to be accused by Abigail. The terrifying thing is that the court believes everything Abigail says.

CHECKPOINT 14 It reinforces Hale's doubts about the girls' testimony. Try to find evidence of Hale's doubts.

CHECKPOINT 15 John Proctor is widely respected. Can you find evidence of this in the play?

CHECKPOINT 16 Hale's cowardice is shown when he refuses to act upon his own suspicions. Where else is Hale seen to be weak?

CHECKPOINT 17 Hathorne is ruthless and small-minded. Identify the other characters that are portrayed negatively.

CHECKPOINT 18 Hathorne insists that anyone who speaks out is doing so to harm the court. This stops Hale from speaking out about the sensible nature of the complaints.

CHECKPOINT 19 Abigail is so confident that she threatens the deputy-governor of the province. How does she recover from this mistake?

CHECKPOINT 20 She realises that Hale is turning the court against her.

CHECKPOINT 21 He has realised that it is not God's work but man's greed and envy that have prevailed in Salem.

CHECKPOINT 22 She knew that she would soon be caught out and fled while there was still time.

CHECKPOINT 23 John will not name anyone else when he confesses. Of course, he ultimately cannot bring himself to sign his own confession.

CHECKPOINT 24 Proctor is ashamed that a frail old woman can accept her fate when he is about to lie in order to save his life.

CHECKPOINT 25 Miller has deliberately used inverted sentences and mirrored the language of the King James Bible.

TEST YOURSELF (ACT I)

1 Susanna Walcott

2 Mrs Putnam

3 Rebecca Nurse

4 Reverend Hale

5 Abigail

6 Betty Parris

7 Abigail

8 Giles Corey and John Proctor

TEST YOURSELF (ACT II)

1 John Proctor

2 Mary Warren

3 Reverend Hale

4 John Proctor

5 Sarah Good

6 Abigail

7 Abigail

TEST YOURSELF (ACT III)

1 Giles Corey

2 Deputy-Governor Danforth

3 Abigail

4 Elizabeth Proctor

5 John Proctor

6 Mary Warren

7 Mary Warren

8 Reverend Hale

TEST YOURSELF (ACT IV)

1 Reverend Samuel Parris

2 Reverend Samuel Parris

3 Elizabeth Proctor

4 John Proctor

5 Deputy-Governor Danforth

6 Sarah Good and Tituba

7 Reverend Hale

8 Martha Corey

Maya Angelou
I Know Why the Caged Bird Sings

Jane Austen
Pride and Prejudice

Alan Ayckbourn
Absent Friends

Elizabeth Barrett Browning
Selected Poems

Robert Bolt
A Man for All Seasons

Harold Brighouse
Hobson's Choice

Charlotte Brontë
Jane Eyre

Emily Brontë
Wuthering Heights

Shelagh Delaney
A Taste of Honey

Charles Dickens
David Copperfield
Great Expectations
Hard Times
Oliver Twist

Roddy Doyle
Paddy Clarke Ha Ha Ha

George Eliot
Silas Marner
The Mill on the Floss

Anne Frank
The Diary of a Young Girl

William Golding
Lord of the Flies

Oliver Goldsmith
She Stoops to Conquer

Willis Hall
The Long and the Short and the Tall

Thomas Hardy
Far from the Madding Crowd

The Mayor of Casterbridge
Tess of the d'Urbervilles
The Withered Arm and other Wessex Tales

L.P. Hartley
The Go-Between

Seamus Heaney
Selected Poems

Susan Hill
I'm the King of the Castle

Barry Hines
A Kestrel for a Knave

Louise Lawrence
Children of the Dust

Harper Lee
To Kill a Mockingbird

Laurie Lee
Cider with Rosie

Arthur Miller
The Crucible
A View from the Bridge

Robert O'Brien
Z for Zachariah

Frank O'Connor
My Oedipus Complex and Other Stories

George Orwell
Animal Farm

J.B. Priestley
An Inspector Calls
When We Are Married

Willy Russell
Educating Rita
Our Day Out

J.D. Salinger
The Catcher in the Rye

William Shakespeare
Henry IV Part I
Henry V
Julius Caesar

Macbeth
The Merchant of Venice
A Midsummer Night's Dream
Much Ado About Nothing
Romeo and Juliet
The Tempest
Twelfth Night

George Bernard Shaw
Pygmalion

Mary Shelley
Frankenstein

R.C. Sherriff
Journey's End

Rukshana Smith
Salt on the snow

John Steinbeck
Of Mice and Men

Robert Louis Stevenson
Dr Jekyll and Mr Hyde

Jonathan Swift
Gulliver's Travels

Robert Swindells
Daz 4 Zoe

Mildred D. Taylor
Roll of Thunder, Hear My Cry

Mark Twain
Huckleberry Finn

James Watson
Talking in Whispers

Edith Wharton
Ethan Frome

William Wordsworth
Selected Poems

A Choice of Poets

Mystery Stories of the Nineteenth Century including The Signalman

Nineteenth Century Short Stories

Poetry of the First World War

Six Women Poets

Margaret Atwood
Cat's Eye
The Handmaid's Tale

Jane Austen
Emma
Mansfield Park
Persuasion
Pride and Prejudice
Sense and Sensibility

Alan Bennett
Talking Heads

William Blake
*Songs of Innocence and of
Experience*

Charlotte Brontë
Jane Eyre
Villette

Emily Brontë
Wuthering Heights

Angela Carter
Nights at the Circus

Geoffrey Chaucer
The Franklin's Prologue and Tale
The Miller's Prologue and Tale
*The Prologue to the Canterbury
Tales*
*The Wife of Bath's Prologue and
Tale*

Samuel Coleridge
Selected Poems

Joseph Conrad
Heart of Darkness

Daniel Defoe
Moll Flanders

Charles Dickens
Bleak House
Great Expectations
Hard Times

Emily Dickinson
Selected Poems

John Donne
Selected Poems

Carol Ann Duffy
Selected Poems

George Eliot
Middlemarch
The Mill on the Floss

T.S. Eliot
Selected Poems
The Waste Land

F. Scott Fitzgerald
The Great Gatsby

E.M. Forster
A Passage to India

Brian Friel
Translations

Thomas Hardy
Jude the Obscure
The Mayor of Casterbridge
The Return of the Native
Selected Poems
Tess of the d'Urbervilles

Seamus Heaney
*Selected Poems from 'Opened
Ground'*

Nathaniel Hawthorne
The Scarlet Letter

Homer
The Iliad
The Odyssey

Aldous Huxley
Brave New World

Kazuo Ishiguro
The Remains of the Day

Ben Jonson
The Alchemist

James Joyce
Dubliners

John Keats
Selected Poems

Christopher Marlowe
Doctor Faustus
Edward II

Arthur Miller
Death of a Salesman

John Milton
Paradise Lost Books I & II

Toni Morrison
Beloved

George Orwell
Nineteen Eighty-Four

Sylvia Plath
Selected Poems

Alexander Pope
*Rape of the Lock & Selected
Poems*

William Shakespeare
Antony and Cleopatra
As You Like It
Hamlet
Henry IV Part I
King Lear
Macbeth
Measure for Measure
The Merchant of Venice
A Midsummer Night's Dream
Much Ado About Nothing
Othello
Richard II
Richard III
Romeo and Juliet
The Taming of the Shrew
The Tempest
Twelfth Night
The Winter's Tale

George Bernard Shaw
Saint Joan

Mary Shelley
Frankenstein

Jonathan Swift
*Gulliver's Travels and A Modest
Proposal*

Alfred Tennyson
Selected Poems

Virgil
The Aeneid

Alice Walker
The Color Purple

Oscar Wilde
The Importance of Being Earnest

Tennessee Williams
A Streetcar Named Desire

Jeanette Winterson
Oranges Are Not the Only Fruit

John Webster
The Duchess of Malfi

Virginia Woolf
To the Lighthouse

W.B. Yeats
Selected Poems

Metaphysical Poets